Turbulent Times for Japanese Politics
激動 日本の政治

TAKEUCHI Yuzuru

竹内　譲

中央公論事業出版

Prologue

(December 2022)

The novel coronavirus pandemic, Russia's invasion of Ukraine and the assassination of former Prime Minister ABE Shinzo, these incidents from 2020 to 2022 must be officially recorded in history textbooks in Japan and around the world. Since the outbreak of the novel coronavirus infection, the world has fallen into chaos. Russia's invasion of Ukraine has created both a global security and energy crisis, which has accelerated inflation. The assassination of former Prime Minister ABE still shakes Japanese society. This has been a truly turbulent time, indeed. The aim of this book is to explain the political, economic and social circumstances, and express my thoughts on critical themes that have occurred during this time.

On September 27, 2020, I was appointed as chairperson of the Policy Research Council of the KOMEITO party, which is part of the ruling coalition with the Liberal Democratic Party (LDP).

During this time, I was involved in important decision making for the SUGA and KISHIDA administrations, such as countermeasures for COVID-19 attacking one after another, and budget compilations for fiscal 2021 and 2022, including three supplementary budgets. Furthermore, as policy chief, I mobilized the KOMEITO to formulate our Manifesto for the 2021 general election, as well as the 2022 House of Councillors election. Although this was very hard work, the mission of the policy chief is to create value for society, and I was able to experience true pleasure in realizing various policies.

Political power is indispensable for our society. Aristotle, the great philosopher of ancient Greece, preached through his

序文
（2022年12月）

　新型コロナウイルスの世界的大流行、ロシアによるウクライナ侵略、そして安倍晋三元首相の暗殺。2020年から2022年にかけてのこれらの事件は、日本と世界の歴史教科書の中に、公式に記述されることは間違いないだろう。新型コロナウイルスの発生以来、世界は大混乱に陥った。ロシアによるウクライナ侵略は、世界の安全保障とエネルギーの危機をもたらし、インフレーションを加速している。安倍元首相の暗殺事件は、未だに日本社会を揺るがしている。まさに「激動の時代」である。本書の目的は、この「激動の時代」を取り巻く政治的、経済的、社会的な状況を説明するとともに、この間に生起した重要な問題について私の考えを表明することにある。

　2020年9月27日、私は自民党とともに連立与党の一角を占める公明党の政務調査会長の任を拝命した。この間、次々に襲いかかる新型コロナウイルスへの対策、3回の補正予算を含む2021年と2022年の予算編成など、菅義偉、岸田文雄政権の重要な意思決定に関与することとなった。さらには、政務調査会長として、公明党の総力をあげて2021年の衆議院総選挙、2022年の参議院選挙のマニフェストを策定した。これは相当な激務であったが、しかし、政務調査会長の使命は「社会に価値を創造すること」であり、様々な政策を実現する醍醐味を体験させて頂くことができた。

　政治権力は、我々の社会には無くてはならないものである。古代ギリシアの偉大な哲学者、アリストテレスは著書『ニコマコス倫理学』の中で、「政治の目的は、人類の最高善を追求することである」と述べている。

3

"*Nicomachean Ethics*" that the purpose of politics is to pursue the supreme good for the human race.

However, whether democracy or autocracy, a person in authority or an authoritarian nation can become arrogant and possessed by the devil of power. Innumerable politicians both in the East and the West were consumed by the devil of power and destroyed their careers. Russia's invasion of Ukraine is an obvious abuse of power by a dictator. This also applies to erratic missile launches by North Korea. China's authoritarian behavior has caused many conflicts regarding territory and economic security with international societies.

In any case, it is crucial to prevent the abuse of power, otherwise, it will bring about the oppression of human rights, wars, plagues and unhappiness. In order to prevent an abuse of power, it is generally said that democracy is superior to autocracy. However, if autocracy is connoted within a democratic nation, serious problems will occur. Modern society including every institution, needs to construct a system to control the despotism of power. Furthermore, it is no exaggeration to say that politicians must be careful with the devil of power which tempts them to commit sins. Without a solid bedrock of ethics, any politician could easily surrender themselves to this power. Ethics is a prerequisite condition for a politician.

In this book, I have tried to unveil the nature of political power through the analysis for global issues as well as domestic affairs. Furthermore, I stressed how the KOMEITO has deliberated and taken action regarding structural agendas such as the declining birth rate, digitalization and decarbonization of Japan.

This collection of essays was written chronologically from 2020 to 2022 in English for overseas readers and later translated into Japanese for this publication to vividly remind Japanese readers of the incidents and agendas of that time. Therefore, this book

しかしながら、民主主義であれ、専制主義であれ、権力者や権威的な国家というものは、傲慢になって権力の魔性に取りつかれることがある。洋の東西を問わず、政治家が権力の魔性に魅入られて、その地位を失った例は枚挙に遑（いとま）がない。ロシアによるウクライナ侵略は、明らかに独裁者による権力の乱用である。これは、常軌を逸したミサイル発射を続けている北朝鮮にも当てはまるものだ。中国の権威主義的行動は、領土や経済安全保障を巡って国際社会と多くの対立を引き起こしている。

　いずれにせよ、権力の乱用を防ぐことが極めて重要である。さもなければ、人権の弾圧、戦争、疫病、そして人々に不幸をもたらすだろう。権力の乱用を防ぐには、一般的には民主主義の方が専制主義よりも優れているとされている。しかし、民主主義国家であっても、その体制の中に専制主義が内包されている場合は、問題が深刻である。現代社会は、あらゆる機関において権力の暴走をコントロールする仕組みを構築することが求められている。さらに政治家は、罪を犯させようと誘惑する「権力の魔性」を警戒しなければならないと言っても過言ではない。固い倫理観の基盤が無ければ、いかなる政治家も簡単に「権力の魔性」に屈服してしまうであろう。倫理は政治家の前提条件である。

　私はこの本の中で、国内問題だけではなく国際的・地球的な問題についての分析を通じて、政治権力の本質を明らかにしようと努めてきたつもりだ。さらに、少子化、デジタル化、脱炭素化などの日本の構造的な課題について、公明党がどのように考え行動してきたかを強調している。

　このエッセー集は、2020年から2022年まで年代順に、海外の読者向けに英語で書いたものだ。当時の出来事や課題について、日本の読者がありありと思い起こすことができるように、後からこの出版のた

could be viewed as a historical document, and used as a reference for future generations. This book is a follow up to my previous book published in English in 2019 entitled "*Japanese Politics One Politician's Perspective: From the DPJ administration to the LDP-KOMEITO ruling coalition (2010-2019)* ".

I would like to express my profound gratitude to Mr. Jason Tonge who proofread my manuscripts and advised me through discussions during these turbulent times.

めに日本語に翻訳した。将来この著作が歴史的な文書とみなされ、参考文献として使われることもあるかもしれない。なお、本書は2019年に上梓した私の英文著書 *"Japanese Politics One Politician's Perspective: From the DPJ administration to the LDP-KOMEITO ruling coalition (2010‒2019)"*、邦題『日本の政治〜ある政治家の視点——民主党政権から自公連立政権へ（2010‒2019）』の続編である。この「激動の時代」に、原稿を校正し、議論を通じて私にアドバイスをしてくださったジェイソン・トンジ氏に心からの感謝を申し上げたい。

Contents 一目次

The Peaks and Valleys of ABE's Long Administration
(January 2020)

As of November 20, 2019, Mr. ABE Shinzo has become the longest serving Prime Minister of Japan. How has Prime Minister ABE retained his administration for such a long time? There are several reasons pointed out by scholars and the media.

The first reason is attributed to the success of "Abenomics", which has dramatically restored Japan's economic condition from deflation. The second is that Mr. ABE has repeatedly dissolved the House of Representatives when the opposition parties were weak and unable to sufficiently prepare for an election. The third is the division within the opposition parties. The now defunct Democratic Party of Japan (DPJ) split into the Constitutional Democratic Party of Japan (CDP), the National Democratic Party (NDP), the Kibo Party and others. Recently, the CDP and NDP started merger negotiations; but according to the press, it doesn't seem likely since many people still recall the recent failure of the DPJ's administration (2009-2012).

However, I believe the most crucial reason is because the KOMEITO bolstered the Liberal Democratic Party (LDP) in both elections and policies, as I stated in my previous book *"Japanese Politics One Politician's Perspective: From the DPJ administration to the LDP-KOMEITO ruling coalition (2010-2019)"*.

His term, however, hasn't been without controversy. Currently, due to the issues surrounding the state cherry-blossom viewing event, the approval rate for ABE's Cabinet has fallen about 10 points over the past two months. Prime Minister ABE has been accused of using this event to entertain about 800 of his supporters. This event has become a thorn in his side as it is

山あり谷ありの安倍長期政権

（2020 年 1 月）

　2019 年 11 月 29 日時点で、安倍晋三首相は、日本で最も在任期間が長い総理大臣となっている。どうして安倍首相は、そのような長期間に亘り政権を維持することができたのか。学者やメディアはいくつかの理由を指摘している。

　第 1 の理由は、アベノミクスの成功に基づくものである。アベノミクスが日本経済の状態を、デフレから劇的に立て直したことである。第 2 の理由は、野党が弱くて、衆議院選挙の準備が十分にできていない時に、繰り返し衆議院を解散したことである。第 3 の理由は、野党の分裂である。かつての民主党は、立憲民主党、国民民主党、そして希望の党などに分裂してしまった。最近になって立憲民主党と国民民主党が合併の交渉を開始したようだが、うまくいくようには見えない。なぜなら、多くの国民が未だに民主党政権の失敗を思い出すからだ。

　しかしながら、私は最も重要な理由は、公明党が自民党を選挙でも政策でも、しっかりと支えているからだと確信している。このことは、私の前回の英文著書である "*Japanese Politics One Politician's Perspective: From the DPJ administration to the LDP-KOMEITO ruling coalition (2010–2019)*"、邦題『日本の政治〜ある政治家の視点──民主党政権から自公連立政権へ（2010–2019）』で述べているとおりだ。

　しかし、安倍首相の任期中は論争が絶えなかった。現在は、「桜を見る会」をめぐる問題で、安倍内閣の支持率はこの 2 カ月間で 10％も落ちている。安倍首相は、約 800 人もの彼の後援会の人々を楽し

funded by taxes every year.

Furthermore, a member of the House of Representatives and a past vice minister of the Cabinet Office, was arrested on suspicion of accepting bribes from a Chinese firm which is bidding to develop Integrated Resort (IR) businesses including casino in Japan. It is reported that this Chinese firm offered funds to several Diet members.

The state cherry-blossom viewing event and IR business will be the most controversial issues in the ordinary Diet session which starts on January 20. The opposition parties will mount a serious attack regarding these matters.

ABE's long administration might have loosened discipline amongst the ruling party members without his notice. The ruling coalition, including the KOMEITO, should tighten the reins on administration management.

UPDATE: As of early January 2020, nobody anticipated that a pneumonia of unknown origin detected in the city of Wuhan, China, will later cause such a pandemic and bring on huge consequences around the world. The Japanese government had made every effort to contain the infection within the Diamond Princess cruise ship.

Prime Minister ABE, the state cherry-blossom viewing event. (Shinjuku Gyoen, Tokyo. Photo: KyodoNews April 13, 2019)
「桜を見る会」であいさつする安倍首相（2019 年 4 月 13 日、東京・新宿御苑、写真＝共同通信社）

ませるために、このイベントを利用したと糾弾されているのだ。この「桜を見る会」は毎年税金で運営されており、安倍政権のとげとなっている。

　さらには、衆議院議員で元内閣府副大臣が、日本でのカジノを含む統合型リゾート（IR）事業の開発を進める中国系企業から、賄賂を受け取った容疑で逮捕された。報道では、その中国系企業は、何人かの国会議員に資金を提供したと伝えられている。

　「桜を見る会」と「IR事業」は、この1月に始まる通常国会において、最も議論となる問題であり、野党はこれらの問題に関して激しい攻撃を加えることになるだろう。

　安倍長期政権は、知らないうちに与党議員の規律を弛緩させてしまったのかもしれない。公明党も含めた連立与党は、政権運営の手綱を引き締めていかなければならない。

（後日談）

　2020年1月の時点では、中国の武漢で発見された原因不明の肺炎が、後にあのような世界的大流行（パンデミック）を引き起こし、世界中に大きな被害をもたらすとは誰も予想していなかった。日本政府は、クルーズ船「ダイヤモンド・プリンセス」号の中に感染を閉じ込めるために、躍起となっていたのである。

696名の感染者と6名の死者が確認されたダイヤモンド・プリンセス号（横浜港、2020年2月）
The Diamond Princess cruise ship, with 696 infections and 6 fatalities confirmed. (Port of Yokohama, February, 2020)

Crucial Issues surrounding Constitutional Amendment
(January 2020)

For his legacy, Prime Minister ABE Shinzo has been eager to amend the Constitution. Specifically, with regards to Article 9, which declares the "Renunciation of War".

The Constitution of Japan was established in 1947 after the Second World War and has yet to be amended. The Constitution describes three major principles; first is the sovereign power of the people, the second is the respect for fundamental human rights, and the third is renunciation of war.

After deep reflection of World War II, many Japanese people find it unnecessary to amend the Constitution. They think that the Constitution has played a key role in maintaining peace for 75 years, and fear that Japan may again be persuaded into war by a Constitutional Amendment.

On the other hand, some people consider that the Constitution of Japan, which was for the most part established by the U.S., is a product of occupation policy by the U.S. forces. They insist that Japan must establish its own Constitution.

Based on these contrasting views, Prime Minister ABE proposes that Article 9, "Renunciation of War", need not be changed, but instead, the role of the Self Defense Forces should be defined.

In order to amend the Constitution of Japan, the Diet must propose a plan to the Japanese people where more than two-thirds of all members from both Houses agree upon. The plan then needs to be approved through a national referendum.

In the Diet, the LDP and the Japan Innovation Party are proponents for Constitutional Amendment; however, the KOMEITO takes a more prudent posture. The rest of the

憲法改正をめぐる重要問題

（2020 年 1 月）

　安倍晋三首相は彼自身の政治的レガシー（遺産）として、憲法改正を実現することに熱心である。とりわけ、「戦争の放棄」を宣言している憲法 9 条である。

　日本国憲法は第二次世界大戦後の 1947 年に施行されたが、まだ一度も改正されたことはない。憲法は 3 つの重要な原則を規定している。すなわち、第 1 に、国民主権。第 2 に、人権の尊重。そして第 3 が、戦争の放棄である。

　第二次世界大戦の深い反省から、多くの日本国民は、憲法改正は不必要であると思っている。また戦後 75 年の間、平和を維持する上で憲法が重要な役割を果たしてきたと考えており、憲法改正によって日本が戦争に引きずり込まれることを恐れている。

　その一方で、一定の人々は、日本国憲法がその大半を米国によって作られたものであり、米軍の占領政策の産物であると見做しているのである。彼らは、日本自身の憲法を制定しなければならないと主張する。

　このような対照的な見解を踏まえて、安倍首相は、「憲法 9 条の『戦争の放棄』は改正の必要は無く、その代わりに自衛隊の役割を憲法に規定するべきである」と提案している。

　日本国憲法を改正するには、国会は衆参両院のすべての国会議員の 3 分の 2 以上の同意を得て、国民に発議しなければならない。発議案は、国民投票を通じて承認される必要がある。

　国会では、自民党と（野党の）日本維新の会が憲法改正に賛成であるが、しかしながら、（与党である）公明党はより慎重な姿勢を取っ

opposition parties are against such an amendment. In the House of Representatives Research Commission on the Constitution, discussions have taken place for a long time, but have now been suspended.

The LDP and the Japan Restoration Party do not have a two-thirds majority in both Houses. Therefore, the KOMEITO holds the key to unlock this stalemate.

Essentially, the Japanese people appreciate the roles and activities of the Self Defense Forces(SDF); however, there are some scholars that regard the SDF as unconstitutional. The KOMEITO regards the SDF as constitutional, but I worry that if the SDF is defined in Article 9, the interpretation of Article 9 may be changed.

To date, under Article 9 of the Constitution, Japan has the right to self-defense, but is only allowed to exercise the right to collective self-defense in a limited capacity. However, defining the SDF in Article 9 may lead to a full allowance on the right to exercise collective self-defense.

Given the significant importance of this matter, further discussions are needed in the Research Commission on the Constitution in both Houses.

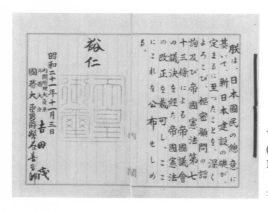

The original Constitution of Japan. (November 3, 1946. Collection, the National Archives of Japan)
日本国憲法・御署名原本（昭和21年11月3日、国立公文書館蔵）

ている。他の野党は改正に反対である。衆議院の憲法調査会では、長い間議論が行われてきたが、しかし現在は中断している。

　自民党と日本維新の会だけでは、両議院の3分の2の議席を有していない。したがって、公明党がこの行き詰まりを打開する鍵を担っているのである。

　基本的には、日本国民は自衛隊の役割や活動を高く評価している。しかしながら、多くの学者たちは自衛隊を憲法違反とみなしているのだ。公明党は、自衛隊を合憲と考えているが、しかし、もしも自衛隊が憲法9条に規定されたならば、憲法9条の解釈が変更されるかもしれないと、私は懸念している。

　今日まで、憲法9条のもとでは、日本は自衛権を有してはいるが、集団的自衛権は限定的に行使することが認められているだけだ。しかしながら、憲法9条に自衛隊を明記することによって、集団的自衛権の行使を全面的に容認することになるかもしれないのである。

　この問題の著しい重要性に鑑みると、国会の両議院の憲法調査会におけるさらなる議論が必要であろう。

国会議事堂（東京）
The National Diet Building, Tokyo.

Fierce Battle for the 2020 Kyoto City Mayoral Election
(January 2020)

Time and time again, Kyoto City mayoral elections have been fierce battles between candidates recommended by the ruling bloc of the Kyoto City assembly and by the Japan Communist Party (JCP).

At present, the fixed membership of the Kyoto City assembly is 67. The ruling bloc, which consists of 21 Liberal Democratic Party (LDP) members, 10 from the KOMEITO, and 6 from the Democratic Civil Forum (DCF), while the opposition bloc is made up of 19 from the JCP, 5 from the Kyoto Party (local party), and 11 from others.

During the chaotic post-war period, the JCP gained favor in Kyoto Prefecture and were able to win the first post-war gubernatorial election. Mr. NINAGAWA Torazo, backed by the JCP, had continued winning elections, serving seven terms and spent 28 years as the governor of Kyoto Prefecture. Under this advantageous circumstance, the JCP founded many hospitals, welfare facilities, labor unions, and associations of commerce and industry. This is how the JCP established their power in Kyoto City.

The 2020 Kyoto City mayoral election is from January 19 to February 2. This time, three candidates will run for mayor; Mr. KADOKAWA Daisaku, the incumbent mayor, and two newcomers from the JCP and the Kyoto Party.

The Kyoto Party candidate is younger (41), proposing reform policies that could siphon support from the incumbent mayor. As a consequence, the possibility of the JCP's win has come to the forefront.

大激戦の 2020 年京都市長選挙

（2020 年 1 月）

　これまで何度も、京都市長選挙は京都市議会の与党の推薦候補者と、日本共産党との激しい戦いであった。

　現在、京都市議会の定数は 67 である。市議会の与党は、自民党が 21 議席、公明党が 10 議席、民主市民フォーラムが 6 議席であるが、野党は、日本共産党が 19 議席、京都党が 5 議席、その他が 11 議席となっている。

　戦後の混乱期に、日本共産党は京都府で人気を博し、戦後最初の知事選挙を勝利することができた。日本共産党が丸抱えした蜷川虎三氏が、その後も勝利を続け、7 期、28 年もの間、京都府知事を務めたのである。このような有利な状況のもとで、日本共産党は、多くの病院、福祉施設、労働組合、そして商工団体などを設立した。こうして、日本共産党は京都市でその勢力を確立したのである。

　2020 年の京都市長選挙は、1 月 19 日から 2 月 2 日まで行われる予定だが、今回は、現職の門川大作氏と、日本共産党と京都党の新人 2 名の、計 3 名が立候補した。

　京都党の候補者は 41 歳と若く、現職市長から支持者を吸い上げるかもしれない改革政策を提唱している。その結果、日本共産党が勝利する可能性が出てきた。

　京都市は、西暦 794 年から 1868 年まで日本の首都であったので、国宝や世界遺産を含む神社仏閣など、多くの歴史的建造物で有名である。もしも、2020 年の京都市長選挙で日本共産党が勝利することになれば、それは「共産主義革命」と言っても過言ではないだろう。

　現職の門川市長は、自民党、公明党、国民民主党、立憲民主党、社

Kyoto City is the former capital of Japan (794 ~1868A.D.), and is famous for its many historical architectural designs such as temples and shrines, which include national treasures and world heritages. If the JCP prevails in the 2020 Kyoto City mayoral election, it would be no exaggeration to say "Communist Revolution".

The incumbent, Mr. KADOKAWA is endorsed by the LDP, KOMEITO, NDP, CDP and SDP, and the JCP criticizes our coalition as a "five-party backing". Surely, in the Diet, the LDP and KOMEITO are the ruling bloc, whereas, the NDP, CDP and SDP are the opposition.

On the other hand, the purpose of local autonomy is to improve people's welfare. From this point of view, it is both reasonable and practical to think that both the ruling parties and the opposition in the Diet can support the same mayor in local politics. We must not fail to win this election.

UPDATE: The incumbent mayor, Mr. KADOKAWA won the election on February 2. The candidate backed by the JCP and REIWA Party was defeated; however, these two parties unprecedentedly expanded their election campaigns by including social media. Their use of Twitter was especially clever and powerful, which affected a younger generation of voters. As the ruling party, we also have to research the best way of using various internet tools for future election campaigns.

Mr. KADOKAWA won the election, February 2, 2020.

民党から推薦を受けているので、日本共産党は我々の連立を「5 党相乗り」だと批判している。確かに、国会では、自民党と公明党が与党であるが、国民民主党、立憲民主党、そして社民党は野党なのである。

　他方で、地方自治の目的は、住民福祉の向上にある。この観点からすると、国会での与党と野党が、地方政治において同じ市長を応援できると考えることは、合理的であり、かつ実際的なのである。我々は、今回の選挙に負けるわけにはいかないのだ。

（後日談）

　現職の門川市長は 2 月 2 日に勝利することができた。日本共産党と令和党の支援を受けた候補者は敗れた。しかしこの 2 つの政党は、ソーシャルメディアを使って、前代未聞の大規模な選挙戦を展開したのである。彼らのツイッターの使用は、大変巧みでパワフルであったので、若い世代の有権者に影響を与えた。与党として我々もまた、将来の選挙戦のために、様々なインターネットツールを使いこなす最も良い方法を研究しなければならない。

門川大作氏の選挙活動
Mr. KADOKAWA Daisaku,
the 2020 Kyoto City mayoral
election campaign.

From the Centralized government to a Decentralized nation

In 1868, the capital city of Japan was said to be relocated from Kyoto to Tokyo. However, as the Meiji Emperor at the time didn't announce the order for the relocation of the capital, Tokyo was not officially recognized as such.

Although the Pacific War, in 1945, resulted in a nation in ruin, the concentration of all aspects of Japanese society was further advanced in Tokyo from the post war to the present time.

No one can deny that Japanese society has currently been in a deadlock and enveloped in disenchantment, which is symbolized by the serious declining birth rate. On the other hand, in provincial areas, there are many hidden opportunities for development such as the beautiful nature, clear air and water, cheap price of lands, heritages and so forth; but no human resources and jobs.

We stand at a turning point of civilization. I think that we should convert the centralized government to a decentralized nation which comprises a federal government and 47 states, and advance the drastic devolution of authority to local governments, and the relocation of the capital and central government agencies. It seems to me that there is a chance given to us by the novel coronavirus pandemic. Germany has achieved its modernization as a decentralized nation while keeping its natural environment. Centralized government is not necessarily a prerequisite condition for modernization.

In March 2023, the Agency for Cultural Affairs is set to relocate

from Tokyo to Kyoto. This is the first time for central government agencies to relocate from Tokyo to local areas since Meiji era. I hope a further decentralization in the future.

Kyoto Imperial Palace
京都御所

中央集権国家から地方分権型国家へ

　1868年、日本の首都は京都から東京へと移ったとされている。ところが、当時の明治天皇は東京遷都の詔を発出していなかった。したがって、東京は公式には首都ではなく、明治以来の慣行に過ぎないのだ。

　1945年、太平洋戦争は国家の破滅に至ったが、その後も現在に至るまで東京への一極集中がさらに進んでいる。現在の日本社会が行き詰まり、閉塞感に覆われていることは誰も否定することはできない。深刻な少子化がそれを象徴している。一方で、地方では美しい自然、きれいな空気と水、安価な土地、歴史的遺産など、発展のための多くの潜在的能力がある。但し無いのは、人と仕事である。

　我々は文明の転換点に立っている。私は、中央集権国家から、連邦政府と47州から成る地方分権型国家へと転換し、地方政府への大幅な権限移譲、首都移転や中央省庁の再配置を進めるべきだと考えている。それは、新型コロナウイルスのパンデミックが与えてくれたチャンスのように思える。ドイツは自然環境を保持しながら、地方分権型国家として近代化を成し遂げている。中央集権国家が必ずしも近代化の前提条件とは言えないのである。

　2023年3月、文化庁が東京から京都に移転されることとなった。これは明治維新以来、初めての中央官庁の移転である。今後、一層の地方分権が進むことを期待したい。

高御座（京都御所）
Takamikura is the special Imperial throne which designates the official place where the Emperor sits. Kyoto Imperial Palace.

My Diplomatic Activities
—A visit from U.S. assembly members, and my visit to the European Parliament
(February 2020)

In October 2019, I was appointed manager of the foreign policies department of the KOMEITO, and as director of the committee on foreign affairs in the House of Representatives. On October 28, I also released my new book *"Japanese Politics One Politician's Perspective"* and held book launch parties in Kyoto City and Tokyo.

On November 19, a bipartisan delegation of U.S. State Assembly members from the Republican and Democratic Parties visited the KOMEITO Headquarters in Tokyo. They expressed interest in the KOMEITO as a ruling bloc, and inquired on the fundamental principles, policies, achievements, and the relationship between the KOMEITO and the Liberal Democratic Party (LDP).

They also showed interest in the North Korea abduction issue and asked me if the abductees were taken from foreign countries. I explained that all but one were abducted in Japan. In particular, I told them about YOKOTA Megumi, a girl of thirteen who was abducted on her way home from school in Niigata Prefecture in 1977. This was a violation of human rights and Japan's sovereignty. They were very much surprised by the story.

Next, from November 26 to 28, I visited the European Parliament in Strasbourg, France as a delegation member for parliamentary interaction between Japan and the EU. On November 27, the plenary session of the European parliament was held and Ms. Ursula Gertrud von der Leyen was elected as the first female President of the European Commission. We, the Japanese members which included the LDP and other members, participated in this historical plenary session and were introduced

私の外交活動
──米国議会議員の来日と私の欧州議会訪問
（2020 年 2 月）

　2019 年 10 月、私は公明党の外交部会長と、衆議院外務委員会の理事を拝命した。10 月 28 日には、私は（英語で綴った）新著 "*Japanese Politics One Politician's Perspective*"、邦題『日本の政治 ～ある政治家の視点』が完成し、東京と京都で出版記念会も開催させて頂いた。

　11 月 19 日には、米国の共和党と民主党の議会議員代表団が、東京の公明党本部を訪問。彼らは、与党としての公明党に関心を表明しており、党の基本哲学や政策、実績、そして自民党との関係などについて詳しく尋ねてきた。

　代表団のメンバーは、また北朝鮮の拉致問題についても関心があり、（党の拉致問題対策委員長である）私に対して、「拉致被害者は、外国で拉致されたのか」との質問があった。私は、「17 人の内の 1 人を除いて、ほとんどが日本で拉致された。とりわけ、1977 年、当時 13 歳であった横田めぐみさんは、新潟県で学校からの帰り道で拉致された。これは人権侵害であり主権侵害である」と語ったところ、彼らはこの話に大変驚いた様子だった。

　さらに、11 月 26 日から 28 日まで、私は日本と EU（欧州連合）の議会交流の代表団の 1 人として、フランスのストラスブールにある欧州会議を訪問した。11 月 27 日には、欧州議会の本会議が開催され、ウルズラ・ゲルトルート・フォン・デア・ライエン女史が、欧州委員会の初の女性委員長として選出されたのである。私と、自民党やその他のメンバーを含む日本の代表団は、この歴史的な本会議に参加

as Japanese Diet members.

Our delegation met many VIPs of the European Commission and had major conferences with the European Parliament members. We could reach a common recognition in the importance of "Sustainable Development Goals (SDGs)", such as global warming, eradicating poverty, zero starvation and so forth. There was also valuable agreement that the EU and Japan were politically stable owing to the ability to compromise by their leaders.

I had the opportunity to address conference members regarding the North Korea military crisis and abduction issues. The European Parliament members appreciated my explanation on these issues and of Japan's stance, saying "Japan is exposed to the threat of nuclear weapons and ballistic missiles from North Korea". Furthermore, they said that "The EU can't tolerate such a crime against the Japanese people by North Korea and intends to further cooperate with Japan. The Japanese abductees were no threat to North Korea, nor were they running away from home. There are serious human rights issues in North Korea. However, the international society seems unable to respond to these issues. In the future, the international community needs to put more pressure on North Korea". I fully realized the importance in explaining the North Korea military crises and abduction issues to an international society, which I hope will lead to a resolution.

Strasbourg is a very beautiful and historical city, and I wanted to have a chance to see the sights, but unfortunately, I had to return to Japan right after the conference.

A visit from U.S. State Assembly members to KOMEITO Headquarters, Tokyo, November 2019.

することができ、（欧州議会の全議員の前で）紹介をして頂いた。

　私たち代表団は、欧州委員会の多くの重要人物と会い、欧州議会議員と主要な会議を行ったが、私たちは、地球温暖化、貧困の根絶、飢餓ゼロなどSDGs（持続可能な開発目標）の重要性について、共通の認識に至ることができた。そこではまた、日本とEUは、それぞれのリーダーたちの「妥協する能力」のおかげで、政治的に安定しているという価値ある意見の合致もみたのである。

　私は、北朝鮮の軍事的危機と拉致問題について演説する機会を得た。欧州議会議員たちは、この問題と日本の立場についての私の説明を高く評価し、次のように述べた。すなわち「日本は、北朝鮮による核とミサイルの脅威にさらされている。」さらに「EUは、北朝鮮による日本人に対する、そのような（拉致）犯罪を容認することはできない。（この問題解決のために）日本とさらなる協力をするつもりである。日本人拉致被害者は、北朝鮮に何らの脅威ももたらしてはいない。家出をしたわけでもない。北朝鮮では深刻な人権問題がある。しかしながら、国際社会はこの問題に対応することができていないように見える。将来、国際社会は北朝鮮に対して、より圧力を加える必要がある」と。私は、国際社会に対して、北朝鮮の軍事的危機と拉致問題について説明することの重要性を痛感した。これが問題解決につながることを期待している。

　ストラスブールは大変美しく、歴史的な街である。私は見学をする機会を持ちたいと思ったが、残念ながら会議の後、直ちに日本へ帰らなければならなかったのである。

欧州議会への訪問（ストラスブール、
2019年11月）
My visit to the European Parliament,
Strasbourg, November 2019.

The Novel Coronavirus Pandemic (1)
—A deadly virus emerges
(March 2020)

Recently, a pneumonia of unknown origin had been detected in the city of Wuhan. China first reported the disease to the World Health Organization (WHO) on December 31, 2019. Subsequently, it has rapidly spread across the rest of the world. The WHO declared this outbreak "A Public Health Emergency of International Concern" on January 30, 2020. Then, on February 11, the WHO announced the official name for the new coronavirus disease: COVID-19.

As of March 11, 2020, throughout the world, infections have topped 118, 000 people in 114 countries, with a death toll over 4,200. Specifically, China, Italy, Iran and South Korea have been seriously affected, and these four countries account for over 90% of infections around the world. As a consequence, the WHO finally characterized COVID-19 as a "Pandemic". Currently, in Japan, there have been 568 reported infections and 12 fatalities. Furthermore, among passengers of the Diamond Princess cruise ship, 696 infections and 6 fatalities have been confirmed.

Based on these circumstances, Prime Minister ABE Shinzo on February 27 requested all elementary, junior and senior high schools to close from March 2 until spring vacation which will start in late March. This is an unprecedented situation. Needless to say, both the government and the ruling bloc, the LDP and KOMEITO, have taken various countermeasures against COVID-19 since its onset. However, Mr. ABE made the decision that the next two weeks are very important to curb further expansion of this disease.

The outbreak of COVID-19 has raised questions about China's public hygiene and medical care system. China has expanded economic and military policies over public hygiene, which resulted in

新型コロナウイルスの世界的大流行（1）
——恐るべきウイルスが出現した
（2020 年 3 月）

　最近、中国の武漢で原因不明の肺炎が発見された。中国は 2019 年 12 月 31 日、最初に世界保健機関（WHO）にこの病気を報告したが、その後この病気は急速に世界中に広がっていった。WHO は 2020 年 1 月 30 日に、この病気の発生を「国際的に懸念される公衆衛生上の緊急事態」として発表し、2 月 11 日にはこの新型コロナウイルスによる病気の公式名を COVID-19 と命名したのである。

　2020 年の 3 月 11 日の時点では、世界の感染者数は 114 カ国で 11 万 8,000 人を超え、死者数は 4,200 人以上となっている。とりわけ、中国、イタリア、イラン、韓国の感染状況は深刻であり、この 4 カ国で世界の感染者数の 90% 以上を占めている。その結果、WHO はとうとう COVID-19 の流行を「パンデミック（世界的大流行）」と位置付けた。現在日本では、568 人の感染者数と 12 人の死者数が報告されている。さらに、クルーズ船ダイヤモンド・プリンセス号では、696 人の感染者と 6 人の死者が確認されている。

　このような状況に鑑み、安倍晋三首相は 2 月 27 日、すべての小中高の学校に 3 月 2 日から春休みまでの休校を要請した。これは前代未聞の事態である。言うまでもなく、政府と与党である自民党、公明党も COVID-19 の発生以来様々な対策を取ってきた。しかしながら、安倍首相は、この病気のさらなる蔓延を抑えるためには次の 2 週間が大変重要であるという決断をしたのである。

　COVID-19 の発生は、中国の公衆衛生と医療体制について疑問を投げかけている。中国はこれまで経済や軍事政策を、公衆衛生よりも優先して拡大してきたが、その結果、公衆衛生は不十分なままである。

insufficiencies for public hygiene. It is urgent for China to improve public hygiene including waterworks and sewer systems in the inland areas.

The epidemic of COVID-19 around the world is due to delays in response of the Wuhan government. However, essentially, this was caused by the excessive concentration of power and restrictions against critical remarks of the government. If the government of China fails to control the COVID-19 epidemic, the international society will lose trust in China and this will change the relationship with China for many countries.

Incidentally, the Japanese government has already requested people to suspend or postpone large scale events and gatherings. Furthermore, public offices and private companies have adopted telecommuting as one of the countermeasures against COVID-19. This has been very effective in preventing this disease from spreading further. In Tokyo, many people commute to work on crowded trains every day. We need to change working styles and education to teleworking and online learning in the future.

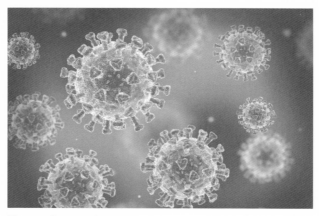

The novel coronavirus

中国にとっては、内陸部の水道や下水道を含む公衆衛生を改善することが急務である。

　世界における COVID-19 の流行は、武漢政府の対応の遅れが原因である。しかしながら、根本的には、（中央政府への）過度の権力集中と、政府に対する厳しい批判を規制してきたことが招いたと言える。もしも、中国政府が COVID-19 のコントロールに失敗するようなことになれば、国際社会は中国に対する信頼を失い、中国との関係を見直すことになるだろう。

　ところで、日本政府はすでに大規模なイベントや集会を延期するように要請している。さらに、公的機関や民間企業はコロナウイルス対策としてテレワークを始めているが、これはさらなる蔓延を防ぐためには大変有効である。東京では多くの人々が毎日満員電車で通勤しているが、今後、働き方や教育をテレワークやオンライン授業に変えていく必要があるだろう。

コロナ禍の静まり返った街の様子
A city silenced amid the novel coronavirus pandemic.

The Novel Coronavirus Pandemic (2)
—The world has fallen into chaos
(April 2020)

The U.S. President Donald Trump declared a "National Emergency" due to the novel coronavirus (COVID-19) global pandemic on March 13 2020, with more than 2,700 confirmed cases and at least 58 reported deaths. At the moment, Europe is the center of the pandemic. Specifically Italy, where COVID-19 infections have exploded and as a consequence, it has been reported that their medical system has collapsed. In Japan, the medical system has prioritized severe COVID-19 patients, which has resulted in curbing an epidemic thus far.

The Trump administration issued new travel restrictions on Europe. Moreover, ABC news reported that "President Trump announced new stricter guidelines to stop the spread of the disease. The new nationwide guidelines call on Americans to avoid gatherings of more than 10 people; avoid eating and drinking in bars, restaurants, and public food courts; and encouraging schooling from home across the country, which applies only to the next 15 days."

As a consequence, the Dow Jones index has wildly fluctuated with nosedives and upswings, and for the Tokyo Stock Market Exchange, the Nikkei 225 has plunged around 5 thousand points (-22%) in the last month. For the time being, the world's economies will continue to deteriorate due to the spread of COVID-19.

As for economic policies to combat recession derived from the COVID-19 pandemic, each nation will need to implement various measures, such as providing adequate funds to their money markets, cutting long and short term rates, purchasing a wide range of financial assets, new public works focused on hygiene,

新型コロナウイルスの世界的大流行（2）
——世界は大混乱に陥った
（2020 年 4 月）

　米国のドナルド・トランプ大統領は、2020 年 3 月 13 日、新型コロナウイルスの世界的大流行によって、米国で 2,700 人の感染者と 58 名の死者が確認されたことから、「国家緊急事態」を宣言した。現在、世界的大流行の中心はヨーロッパである。とりわけ、イタリアでは新型コロナウイルスの感染が爆発的に拡大しており、その結果、医療体制が崩壊していると報道されている。日本では、重症患者が死亡するのを防ぐことに重点をおいてきたが、それによって今日まで感染が抑えられている。

　トランプ政権は、ヨーロッパに対する新しい旅行制限を打ち出した。さらに、ABC ニュースは、「トランプ大統領が病気の蔓延を止めるために、新たに厳しいガイドラインを発表。それは 10 人以上の集会を避けるように国民に求めるとともに、バーやレストラン、フードコートでの飲食を避けること、家庭での学習を勧める内容で、次の 15 日間適用される」と伝えている。

　その結果、ダウ・ジョーンズの株式指標は、急落と急騰の激しい変動となっており、また東京証券取引所の日経 225 は、1 カ月で約 5,000 円（22%）も急落した。当面の間、世界経済は新型コロナウイルスの拡大によって悪化が続くであろう。

　新型コロナウイルスの世界的大流行による景気後退と戦う経済政策については、各国とも様々な手段を実行する必要があり、例えば市場への十分な資金の供給、長短期の金利の引き下げ、幅広い金融資産の購入、公衆衛生に的を絞った公共事業、減税などである。

　3 月 14 日には、安倍晋三首相は「政権として新型コロナウイルス

reducing taxes and so on.

On March 14, Prime Minister ABE Shinzo announced that his administration will make the utmost effort in preventing a COVID-19 epidemic, and boldly take economic and financial measures to stabilize the Japanese economy as soon as possible with unprecedented creativity.

Many people are paying close attention on whether the government will reduce the consumption tax rate. However, this tax revenue is used to maintain Japan's social security system, and it would be very difficult to raise these rate again after the pandemic subsides. The most crucial issue for Japan is whether the Tokyo Olympics and Paralympics can be held. President Trump commented on the possibility of postponement until next year, which swayed the Japanese government and people. It will of course depend on the circumstances of the COVID-19 pandemic; however, on March 24, Prime Minister ABE announced a one year postponement through negotiations with President Bach of the International Olympic Committee.

Newly updated countdown (top) for the 2021 Tokyo Olympics and Paralympics after postponement. (Big screen, Shinbashi Tokyo, Photo: KyodoNews) 「東京五輪延期決定1ヵ月」東京2020組織委員会、仕切り直しの準備——東京オリンピック・パラリンピックまでの新たな残り日数が表示された大型画面（上）（東京・新橋駅前、写真＝共同通信社）

の流行を防ぐために最大限の努力を行うこと、また日本経済をできる限り早く安定化させるために、かつてない発想で大胆に経済・金融の手段を講じる」と発表した。

　多くの国民は、政府が消費税を引き下げるかどうかに注目している。しかしながら、消費税収は日本の社会保障を維持するために使われており、この世界的大流行が収束した後に、再び引き上げることは難しいと思われる。日本にとって最も重大な案件は、東京オリンピック・パラリンピックが開催できるかどうかである。トランプ大統領は来年までの延期の可能性に言及したが、これは日本政府と国民を揺さぶっている。もちろん、それは新型コロナウイルスの世界的大流行の状況次第である。しかし、安倍首相は国際オリンピック委員会のバッハ会長との協議を経て、3月24日に1年延期を発表したのである。

IOC バッハ会長と電話会談する安倍首相（右から3人目）。右から菅官房長官、大会組織委員会の森会長。左手前から橋本五輪相、東京都の小池知事（2020年3月24日、首相公邸、内閣広報室写真＝共同通信社）
Prime Minister ABE, meeting with President Bach of the IOC by phone. (Prime minister's office, Photo: KyodoNews, March 24, 2020)

The Novel Coronavirus Pandemic (3)
—State of emergency in Japan
（April 2020）

As of April 11, coronavirus infections around the world topped 1.5 million people in 185 countries, with a death toll over 100,000. One month earlier, on March 11, the number of cases were around 119,000, with fatalities near 4,300. This disease broke out in Wuhan, China last December and has rapidly spread throughout the world. As a consequence, it has become an unprecedented catastrophe.

Specifically in the U.S., where the number of cases topped 500,000, with over 18,000 fatalities, making it the worst affected country in the world. It has been reported that the medical system in the U.S., Italy, Spain and France, have already collapsed due to an "Overshoot"—meaning an explosion in infections that doubles every two or three days. These nations have implemented "Lockdowns" which is a containment strategy for specific areas and cities. However, it will take a while before this policy is deemed effective.

On April 7, Prime Minister ABE Shinzo finally declared a "state of emergency" for 7 prefectures (Tokyo, Kanagawa, Saitama, Chiba, Osaka, Hyogo and Fukuoka), beginning April 7 until May 6 based on a newly enacted emergency law. This law is intended to suppress a sharp increase of cases, in particular, those of unknown transmission routes.

As of today, there are 5,902 confirmed cases and 94 fatalities in Japan. Although this is not necessarily as bad as the U.S. or Europe, Mr. ABE announced the emergency to prevent Japan's medical system from collapsing.

In accordance with advice of epidemiologists, Mr. ABE requested

新型コロナウイルスの世界的大流行（3）
──日本に緊急事態宣言が発令
（2020 年 4 月）

　4 月 11 日現在、世界 185 カ国で新型コロナウイルスの感染者が150 万人を突破し、死者数は 10 万人を超えている。1 カ月前の 3 月 11 日では、世界の感染者数は約 11 万 9,000 人で、死者数は約4,300 人であった。この病気は 2019 年 12 月に中国の武漢で発生して以来、世界中に急速に広がっており、その結果、前代未聞の大惨事となっている。

　特に米国では、感染者数が 50 万人を超え、1 万 8,000 人以上の死者が出て、世界で最悪の影響を受けた国となっている。米国、イタリア、スペイン、フランスの医療システムは、すでに「オーバーシュート」のために崩壊していると伝えられている。このオーバーシュートとは、2 〜 3 日ごとに感染者数が倍増する爆発的状態を意味する。これらの国々では、特定の地域や都市を封じ込める戦略「ロックダウン」を実施しているが、しかし、この政策が効果を発揮するまでには、しばらくの時間が掛かるであろう。

　4 月 7 日、安倍晋三首相はついに、新たに制定された緊急事態法に基づき、東京都、神奈川県、埼玉県、千葉県、大阪府、兵庫県、福岡県の 7 都府県に対して 4 月 7 日から 5 月 6 日までの緊急事態宣言を発出した。この法律は、感染者の急増、なかでも感染経路不明者の急増を抑えるためのものである。

　今日の時点で、日本では 5,902 名の感染者と 94 名の死者が出ている。これは必ずしも米国や欧州ほど悪い状況ではないが、安倍首相は、日本の医療システムが崩壊するのを防ぐために、緊急事態を宣言したのだ。

people to reduce 70 to 80% of contact with others, and avoid the 3Cs, that is crowded spaces with poor ventilation, crowded conditions, and conversations in close proximity.

Mr. ABE underlines this "Social Distancing" as an important countermeasure against COVID-19. "Social Distancing" usually means keeping 2 meters apart from everyone.

Tokyo Metropolitan governor, KOIKE Yuriko states that Tokyo is on the brink of crisis regarding "Overshoot". She requested citizens to stay at home, and business sectors to close their stores except those necessary for daily living from April 11 until May 6.

However, these countermeasures for this new emergency law are only requests with no enforcement mechanisms. This is attributed to the remorse of wartime fascism that imposed harsh restriction on freedoms. Whether Japan can control the COVID-19 pandemic depends on the self-awareness of every person in Japan.

On the other hand, it is extremely difficult to reduce 80% contact with others. The government should therefore secure sufficient funds to protect people's lives and livelihoods from the COVID-19 threat. We are waging war against the coronavirus pandemic. The government must not hold back funds for fiscal reconstruction.

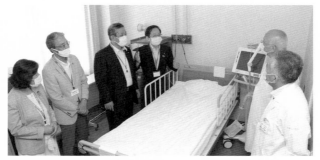

Hospital amid the coronavirus pandemic, 2020. (Kizugawa Hospital, Kyoto Prefecture)
コロナ禍に病院を視察——病院の喫緊の課題などをうかがい、その深刻さを受け止める

感染症学者の助言に従い、安倍首相は国民に対し、他者との接触を70～80%程度減らすとともに、3つの密を避けるように要請した。3つの密とはすなわち、第1に、換気の悪い密閉空間。第2に、密集状態。第3に、近距離での密接な会話である。

安倍首相は、新型コロナウイルスの重要な対抗手段として、この「社会的距離（ソーシャル・ディスタンス）」をとる（3密を避ける）ことを強調。「社会的距離」とは、通常すべての人が2メートル離れることを意味している。

東京都知事の小池百合子（こいけゆりこ）氏は、東京は「オーバーシュート」の瀬戸際の危機にあると述べている。彼女は都民に対して、4月11日から5月6日まで「家にいてください」、また、民間企業には「日常生活で必要な商品を除いて、店舗を休業してください」と要請した。

しかしながら、新しい緊急事態法のこれらの対策は、強制力の無い単なる要請にすぎない。これは、戦時中、人々の自由に対して厳しい制限を課したファシズムの反省に基づくものだ。日本が新型コロナウイルスの世界的大流行をコントロールできるかどうかは、日本人一人ひとりの自覚にかかっているのである。

その一方で、他者との接触を80%低減することは、極めて困難なことである。政府は、したがって十分な資金を確保して、新型コロナウイルスの脅威から人々の命と生活を守らなければならない。我々は新型コロナウイルスの大流行との戦争を闘っている。政府は、財政再建を理由にして、資金の出し惜しみをしてはならない。

Who will win the battle for Global Hegemony - China or the U.S.?
（April 2020）

The conflict between the U.S. and China has further escalated in recent years, which seems to be struggle for hegemony. Prof. KAWASAKI Tsuyoshi from Simon Fraser University insists as follows; "The U.S. represents Western nations which want to maintain the international order of liberalism, and China represents the camps which want to overturn the status quo. After World War II, Western nations led by the U.S. and the U.K. established the international order, where Japan took part in and has obtained security and prosperity for many years. Over 30 years have passed since the end of the Cold War due to the defeat of the Soviet Union, and now the new battle for hegemony has started." (Summary, Nikkei, Inc. February 11, 2020)

Which camp will win, the U.S. or China? The rise of China has surely been impressive. China's development covers various areas such as foreign affairs, military capability, economy, culture, information technology, cyber and space exploration.

However, the *Economist magazine* from the UK says "China has remained under a one-party Communist regime. People are forced to obey the instruction of the Communist Party and their freedom is only guaranteed within the permissible range of the Communist Party. It can be said that Chinese society doesn't permit its people to criticize the government or the Communist Party."

New coronavirus infections have spread from the city of Wuhan to the rest of the world. It has been reported that one Chinese medical doctor revealed this infection threat on social media only to have the Wuhan police authority reprimand him for delivering "false rumors". He subsequently died due to coronavirus infection.

世界の覇権争いを制するのは中国か、それとも米国か
（2020 年 4 月）

　近年、米国と中国の対立は益々エスカレートしており、これは世界の覇権をめぐる闘いの様相を呈している。（カナダの）サイモン・フレイザー大学の川崎 剛 教授は、次のように主張している。すなわち、「米国は、自由主義の国際秩序を維持したい西側諸国を代表しており、中国は現状の秩序を覆したい勢力を代表している。第二次世界大戦後、米国と英国に率いられた西側諸国が国際秩序を確立したが、そこに日本は参加し、長年に亘り安全と繁栄を享受してきた。ソ連の敗北によって冷戦が終了してから 30 年以上が過ぎたが、今新たな覇権争いが始まったのである。」（「日本経済新聞」2020 年 2 月 11 日付）

　米国か中国かどちらの陣営が勝利するのであろうか。中国の台頭は確かに目覚ましかった。中国の発展は外交、軍事力、経済、文化、情報技術、サイバー、宇宙探査計画など様々な分野に亘っている。

　しかしながら、英国の『エコノミスト』誌は、「中国は共産党の一党独裁政権のもとにある。人々は共産党の指導に従わなければならないし、共産党の認める範囲でのみ自由は保障されているに過ぎない。中国社会は、国民に政府や共産党を批判することを許していないと言える」と言う。

　新型コロナウイルスの感染者は、武漢市から世界中に広がっていった。（武漢市の）一人の医師がソーシャルメディアでこの感染の脅威を訴えたが、武漢市警察当局は偽りのうわさを流布したとして、この医師を戒告処分としたのである。その後彼はコロナウイルスの感染によって亡くなった。

　これは、共産党体制の弱点を示しているのかもしれない。行き過ぎ

This may reveal a weakness of the communist regime. The excessive concentration of power does not necessarily protect people's lives. Freedom creates diversity and diversity in turn produces innovation. The restriction on freedoms create obstacles for a sound society.

For the time being, China will continue advancing; however, from a long-term perspective, it is uncertain whether China can overtake the U.S.

To date, the U.S. has engaged China in the ways of Western liberalism and capitalism since the "Economic Reform and Market Economy" policies started in 1978. China has succeeded as an industrialized nation and expanded extensive trade with Western nations. This mutual dependence on trade between China and Western nations has deepened. Therefore, President Donald Trump has no choice but to compromise with China by lowering tariffs on Chinese products.

Nevertheless, since the HUAWEI issue occurred, the U.S. has managed to purge Chinese firms in the arenas of high technology and security. On the other hand, China has absolutely no intention in conceding to Taiwan and matters regarding the South China Sea.

Japan associates itself with Western nations, but the mutual dependence on economy between Japan and China has been intertwined. Therefore, even if conflicts between the U.S. and China intensify, Japan will need to ease tensions between each country. Japan has extended an invitation to Xi Jinping as a state guest in April; however, this will depend on circumstances of the coronavirus epidemic and China's intentions.

In the near future, the population of China will rapidly decline due to their one-child policy and will face a society with seriously fewer children. Given these comprehensive circumstances, China will also need to harmonize with the U.S. and Western nations.

た権力の集中は必ずしも国民の生命を守るとは言えない。自由は多様性を生み、代わりに多様性はイノベーションを創り出す。自由に対する規制は健全な社会の妨げとなる。

　当分の間、中国は発展を続けるであろう。しかしながら、長期的な視点からは、中国が米国に取って代わるかどうかは不確かである。

　今日まで米国は、1978 年の「改革・開放」政策が始まって以来、西側の自由主義と資本主義の中に中国を囲い込もうとしてきた。中国は工業国として成功を収め西側諸国との貿易を拡大し、（その結果）中国と西側諸国との貿易上の相互依存は深まっている。したがって、ドナルド・トランプ大統領は、中国製品に対する関税を低くすることで、中国と妥協するより他はないのだろう。

　それにもかかわらず、ファーウェイ（華為）事件が起きてからは、米国はハイテクや安全保障の分野で、中国企業を（米国市場から）追い出そうと躍起になっている。他方で、中国は、台湾問題や南シナ海にかかわる問題では、譲歩する意図は全く無いのである。

　日本は西側諸国の一員であるものの、しかし、日本と中国との経済の相互依存は深く結びついている。したがって、米国と中国の対立が激化するとしても、日本は両国の緊張を緩和する必要がある。日本は、4 月に予定されていた習近平国家主席の国賓としての招待を延期したところであるが、しかしながら、これが実現するかどうかは、コロナウイルスの流行の状況と中国の出方次第となるであろう。

　近い将来、中国の人口は「一人っ子政策」が原因で急速に減少し、深刻な少子社会に直面することになるだろう。これらの総合的な状況を考慮すると、中国も米国や西側諸国と協調していく必要があると思われる。

UPDATE: After the 2021 general election in October, a conservative Diet member of the LDP visited me, Policy Chief of the KOMEITO, and requested that both Houses should announce a resolution regarding the human rights situation in China. Through deliberations within the KOMEITO then negotiations with the LDP, we created a resolution and proposed it to all of the opposition parties. The major contents are as follows: "International communities are concerned about the seriousness of human rights in Xinjiang Uyghur Autonomous Region, Tibet, Southern Mongolia, and Hong Kong. To change the status-quo by force is considered a threat to international communities. Both Houses strongly require China to fulfill its responsibilities to explain the seriousness of human rights in an acceptable way that the international communities can understand". Subsequently, the Lower House and the Upper House unanimously approved this resolution in February and December 2022, respectively.

（後日談）

　2021年10月の衆院選が終了した後、当時政調会長であった私のもとへ、自民党から、中国の人権問題に関する国会決議を出すべきだという要請があった。そこで、党内の議論や自民党との協議を経て両党で原案を作成し、他のすべての野党にも提示した。その主な内容は以下の通りである。すなわち「国際社会から、新疆ウイグル、チベット、南モンゴル、香港等における深刻な人権状況への懸念が示されている。力による現状の変更を国際社会に対する脅威と認識するとともに、深刻な人権状況について、国際社会が納得するような形で、説明責任を果たすよう強く求める」。その後この決議は、衆議院と参議院において2022年の2月と12月に、それぞれ全会一致で可決された。

米中関係・対立深刻、長期化の懸念——
トランプ米大統領（右）と中国の習近平
国家主席（2017年11月、北京、写真＝
共同通信社）
Concerns regarding the worsening and
prolonged conflicts between the U.S.
and China. (Beijing, Photo: KyodoNews,
November, 2017)

World Politics amid the Pandemic
(May 2020)

Amid the coronavirus pandemic, conflicts between the U.S. and China have further escalated. According to the *Japan Times*, the U.S. claims that a Chinese high-security biosafety center, the Wuhan Institute of Virology (WIV), may be the cradle of the pandemic. The *Washington Post* quoted anonymous sources who voiced concern that the virus may have come accidentally from the facility, and revealed that officials were especially concerned about the inadequate safety at the lab.

On the other hand, China promoted conspiracy theories that the U.S. army may have brought the virus to China. The Chinese government ordered the deportation of American journalists in March, which made international societies harden their attitude toward China. Furthermore, the Chinese government insists that their one-party autocracy is superior to democracy in containing the coronavirus epidemic. However, this propaganda may enhance China's isolation, losing trust around the world.

As of April 30, in the U.S., the number of coronavirus infections topped 1 million, with a death toll 58,000. If this horrible situation continues, the U.S. economy will further decline, and as a consequence, China may supplant the U.S. as the leader of the world's economy.

But would Western nations suffering from the coronavirus pandemic appreciate an authoritarian nation like China? I don't think so. The value of freedom and democracy won't be easily overturned despite Western nations' failures in controlling the explosion of the coronavirus. It can be said that Japan has pursued control of the coronavirus epidemic while respecting human rights as much as

パンデミックの中の世界政治

（2020 年 5 月）

　新型コロナウイルスの世界的大流行（パンデミック）の中で、米国と中国の対立が益々激化している。『ジャパンタイムズ』によると、米国は、高度のセキュリティが保たれている中国のバイオセーフティセンター、武漢ウイルス研究所がパンデミックの発祥の地であると主張している。『ワシントンポスト』は、ウイルスが何らかの事故で施設から漏れ出たのかもしれないと懸念する匿名の情報源を紹介し、研究所員たちが実験室の不十分な安全性を、特に心配していたことを明らかにしている。

　一方で、中国は、米軍が中国にウイルスを持ち込んだ可能性があるという謀略説を流している。中国政府は、3 月に米国のジャーナリストたちの追放を命じたが、そのことが国際社会の中国に対する態度を硬化させることになった。さらには、中国政府は新型コロナウイルスの流行を抑えるには、彼らの一党独裁の方が民主主義よりも優れていると主張しているのである。しかしながら、このプロパガンダは中国の孤立を高め、世界からの信頼を失うことになるかもしれない。

　4 月 30 日の時点で、米国では新型コロナウイルスの感染者数は 100 万人を超え、死者数は 5 万 8,000 人にのぼっている。もしも、この恐ろしい状況が続くならば、米国経済はさらに悪化し、その結果、中国が世界経済のリーダーとして、米国に取って代わるかもしれない。

　しかし、新型コロナウイルスのパンデミックに苦しむ西側諸国が、中国のような権威主義的国家を評価することになるであろうか。私はそうは思わない。西側諸国は、新型コロナウイルスの爆発的感染をコントロールすることに失敗したが、しかしそれでも、自由と民主主義

possible. Democratic nations and areas such as South Korea, New Zealand and Taiwan have reported succeeding in curbing their epidemics.

Professor Dani Rodrik of Harvard University insists that; Whatever excuses U.S. President Donald Trump uses to escape from his responsibility of "Overshoot" in America, this calamity is a crisis that could have been anticipated and ought to be prepared. At first, President Trump made light of the gravity of this crisis. As a consequence, when infections and inpatients rapidly began to increase, a serious situation arose with a shortage of medical materials such as ventilators. (Summary, Nikkei Inc. April 24, 2020)

President Trump denies this point of view and has accused China of spreading the virus around the world. Even if these claims are attributed to the Presidential election in November, China should improve transparency surrounding the coronavirus outbreak and steer towards cooperation with international societies. Nevertheless, the Chinese government has raised the level of nationalism that makes other nations enemies, which will lead to the depreciation of China.

UPDATE: In December 2022, the Chinese government abruptly abandoned the "Zero Coronavirus" policy to completely contain the spread of the coronavirus infection through thorough inspections and severe restrictions on its people, and ordered them to personally take countermeasures against COVID-19. China had formerly appealed that the "Zero Coronavirus" policy showed the supremacy of the Communist Party government. According to the media outlets; it was pointed out that the reason for this change was attributed to the large number of protests that had occurred in late November 2022, as well as a serious economic recession. It's unprecedented that such protests occurred amid the strict restrain

の価値はそう簡単には覆ることはないだろう。日本は人権をできる限り尊重しながら、新型コロナウイルスの流行をコントロールすることを追求してきたと言える。韓国、ニュージーランド、台湾などの民主主義の国と地域は、新型コロナウイルスの流行を抑えることに成功しつつあると伝えている。

　ハーバード大学のダニ・ロドリック教授は、「米国のドナルド・トランプ大統領が、米国におけるオーバシュートの責任から逃れるために、どのように言い訳しようとも、この惨事は初めから予測できたはずであり、また準備すべきであった危機である。最初のうち、トランプ大統領はこの危機の重大性を軽視していた。その結果、感染者と患者が急速に増え始めた時には、人工呼吸器などの医療物資が不足するという深刻な状態が生じたのである」と述べている（要旨「日本経済新聞」2020年4月24日付）。

　トランプ大統領はこの見解を否定し、世界中にウイルスを拡散させた中国を告発している。たとえ、この主張が11月の大統領選挙に起因するとしても、中国は新型コロナウイルスの発生をめぐる透明性を改善し、国際社会との協調の方向に舵を切るべきである。にもかかわらず、中国政府は他国を敵に回すような国家主義のレベルを引き上げている。しかしこれは、結局は中国の評価を下げることになるだろう。

（後日談）

　2022年12月、中国政府は突如、それまでの徹底した検査と人々に対する厳しい行動制限を通じて、完全に新型コロナウイルス感染の拡大を封じ込める「ゼロ・コロナ」政策を放棄し、人々に自己責任での感染対策を命じた。中国は以前「ゼロ・コロナ政策は、中国共産党の統治の優位性を示すものだ」とアピールしていた。報道によると、今回の転換の理由は、深刻な経済不況に加えて、前年11月下旬に起きた数多くの抗

of speech, and criticism was directed towards President Xi Jinping and the Communist Party. As a consequence, it was reported that since early December, the coronavirus infection has immediately expanded across the nation and around 600 million people have contracted COVID-19 among 1,400 million population in China (the infection rate in Pekin exceeded 80%), with many elderly people and those with underlying diseases have died.

Town under the "Zero Coronavirus" policy, China.

議活動が原因であると指摘している。また、厳しい言論統制下での抗議活動や、批判が習近平国家主席や中国共産党に向けられたことも異例である。ゼロ・コロナ政策が放棄された結果、12月上旬以降は全土に感染が急拡大し、中国14億人の内、6億人がすでに罹患（北京での感染率は80％超）、多くの高齢者や基礎疾患のある人々が死亡したと伝えられている。

空港の検疫所
Airport quarantine

Mystery surrounding a Certain Economic Measure
(May 2020)

An unprecedented reorganization of the 2020 supplementary budget was decided by tough negotiations between Prime Minister ABE and the KOMEITO Chief Representative YAMAGUCHI, who is a member of the House of Councillors on April 16, 2020.

The story goes back to March 31. The KOMEITO proposed a plan that the government should dole out ￥100,000 per person to all residents in Japan as an urgent economic countermeasure against the coronavirus pandemic.

However, on April 7, the ABE Cabinet decided on the 2020 supplementary budget which included distributing ￥300,000 to the head of each household who was exempt from local taxes, or who was suffering from more than a 50% decrease in their earnings compared to the previous year due to the coronavirus pandemic. The government reformed the KOMEITO's plan for fiscal reconstruction under pressure of the Ministry of Finance.

Many KOMEITO parliamentary members and their supporters were disappointed to hear the Cabinet's decision. However, soon after the news, innumerable critiques and complaints were directed at not only the government but also the ruling bloc, the LDP and KOMEITO, saying these conditions were very severe and restricted.

On April 14, even the LDP secretary-general, Mr. NIKAI announced that there were imminent voices to support ￥100,000 per person, and he urged the government to implement any countermeasures as soon as possible.

Right after this announcement, Mr. YAMAGUCHI was determined to negotiate with Prime Minister ABE.

According to media outlets, on the morning of April 15, Mr.

YAMAGUCHI spoke to ABE at the Prime Minister's office and required the government to dole out ￥100,000 per person without any conditions. However, Prime Minister ABE only promised to discuss it after enactment of the budget. That afternoon, Mr. YAMAGUCHI called ABE to further request the reorganization of the 2020 supplementary budget as soon as possible. However, ABE refused it, since the 2020 supplementary budget had already been decided by the Cabinet. Nevertheless, the next morning, on April 16, Mr. YAMAGUCHI called ABE by phone to realize the reorganization of the budget. At last, ABE decided to accept the demand from Mr. YAMAGUCHI, despite objections from Finance Minister ASO.

The public were very much surprised and delighted to hear this news.

According to the Ministry of Finance, this reorganization needed to secure another ￥8.8 trillion totaling ￥12 trillion and there has been almost no precedent for such a case. It was a brilliant achievement to make the Cabinet reorganize the decided budget. However, it's not hard to imagine that Mr. YAMAGUCHI had felt enormous pressure. I wonder how Mr. YAMAGUCHI persuaded Prime Minister ABE to overturn the Cabinet decision. It's a mystery. I expect Mr. YAMAGUCHI will tell the tale someday.

The KOMEITO's influence is growing in the ruling coalition. However, the power balance between the government, the LDP and the KOMEITO has become complex. Mr. KISHIDA Fumio was Chairperson of the Policy Research Council of the LDP at that time. Furthermore, an unanticipated problem occurred. It took an extremely long time to distribute ￥100,000 per person to all residents in Japan due to the delay in the "My Number Card". The coronavirus pandemic has unveiled a weak point in the digitalization of Japanese society.

How to consider the snowball effect of national bonds?
(May 2020)

On April 30, the 2020 supplementary budget was enacted in the Diet. Its volume was around ￥25 trillion ($250 billion), which will be procured by issuing national bonds. Financial institutions will bid for the new bonds, while the Bank of Japan (BOJ) is slated to purchase the same volume of national bonds in the market. This is the money easing policy of "Abenomics".

As a consequence, the government can financially rescue individuals, small and medium-sized companies, hospitals and so on from the coronavirus crisis. Similarly, in advanced nations, urgent economic policies accompanied with a huge issuance of national bonds are being adopted as countermeasures against the coronavirus pandemic. As a result, the "Modern Monetary Theory" (MMT) has been gaining attention around the world. (I described MMT in my previous book entitled *"Japanese Politics: One Politician's Perspective"*)

However, the amount of national bonds is approaching ￥1,000 trillion ($10 trillion), with its gross-debt-to GDP (￥535 trillion) ratio for fiscal 2019 around 177%. Major economists fear hyper-inflation attributed to the excessive liquidity of money, while MMT insists that the government can supply money within 3 to 4% inflation. As of today, the inflation rate is below 1% in Japan. Without such vast expenditures by the government against the pandemic, many people may not survive and innumerable corporations could go bankrupt.

The coronavirus pandemic still knows no bounds. As of May 4, around the world, the number of infections topped 3.5 million, with a death toll near 250,000. In Japan, there are 16,385

国債残高の膨張をどう考えるか

（2020 年 5 月）

2020 年 4 月 30 日、第 1 次補正予算が国会で成立した。その規模は約 25 兆円であり、国債を発行して調達されることになる。金融機関は新発債に入札するが、他方で、日本銀行は市場から同額の国債を購入することになる。これは、「アベノミクス」の金融緩和政策である。

その結果、政府はコロナウイルスの危機から、資金的に個人や中小企業、病院などを救うことができる。同様に、先進諸国においても、巨額の国債発行を伴う緊急の経済政策が、コロナウイルスの世界的大流行の対策として採用されつつある。その結果、現代貨幣理論（MMT）が、世界中で注目を集めているのである。（MMT については、私の前著 *"Japanese Politics; One Politician's Perspective"* で述べている）

しかしながら、国債の発行残高は 1,000 兆円に近づいており、2019 年度末の対 GDP（535 兆円）比率は約 177% となっている。主要な経済学者たちは、マネーの過剰な流動性に起因するハイパーインフレーションを恐れているが、他方で MMT は、「政府は、インフレ率が 3 〜 4% の範囲内まではマネーを供給できる」と主張する。現時点では、日本のインフレ率は 1% を下回っている。この世界的大流行のもとで、そのような巨額の歳出が無ければ、多くの人々は生き残ることができず、数えきれないくらいの企業が破産したかもしれない。

新型コロナウイルスの世界的大流行は、未だに留まるところを知らない。5 月 4 日の時点では、世界の感染者の数は 350 万人を超え、死者数は約 25 万人となっている。日本では、現在 1 万 6,385 人の感

confirmed cases and 771 fatalities. On May 7, the ABE Cabinet announced an extension to the state of emergency until May 31, due to the ongoing epidemic.

This will further force individuals and corporations to endure harsh economic conditions. Prime Minister ABE ordered his Cabinet to prepare a second 2020 supplementary budget to protect people's lives and small to medium-sized businesses. The LDP Secretary-general, Mr. NIKAI claimed ￥50 trillion for the second 2020 supplementary budget may be necessary.

Perhaps, the amount of national bonds will further snowball. How will the government reduce such a huge debt? After the pandemic, the Japanese economy will rapidly recover and as a result, tax revenue will increase. If the inflation rate exceeds 3 to 4%, the government may raise tax rates. Nevertheless, it is not easy to reduce the balance of national bonds.

However, government financial assets and the like were around ￥177 trillion in fiscal 2019. Therefore, its net-debt to GDP ratio was around 144%. In looking at this issue from a different perspective, BOJ holds national bonds totaling around ￥500 trillion, which means the virtual balance is around ￥500 trillion.

Furthermore, the estimate for national bonds depends on the credibility of the Japanese economy. Net foreign assets in Japan including the private sector are around ￥350 trillion and the current account balance has kept a huge surplus for a long time. The ratio of foreign investors holding national bonds is just around 7%. Considering the data conprehensivery, it seems to me that the national finances are not necessarily in critical condition. Nevertheless, we need to control inflation. The government should be prudent to issue national bonds while inflation is accelerating.

染者と771人の死者が確認されている。5月7日、安倍内閣は、進行する感染流行を理由として5月31日まで「緊急事態宣言」を延長することを発表した。

　これは、厳しい経済状態の中で、個人や企業にさらに忍耐を強いるものである。そこで安倍首相は、人々の生命と中小企業を守るために、2020年度の第2次補正予算を準備するように内閣に指示を出した。自民党の二階俊博幹事長は、50兆円規模の第2次補正予算が必要だと主張している。

　恐らく、国債の発行残高は雪だるま式に増えていくだろう。政府はどのようにして、そのような巨額の借金を減らしていくのだろうか。世界的大流行の終息後、日本経済は急速に回復し、その結果、税収は増えていくだろう。もしも、インフレ率が3～4%を超えれば、政府は税率の引き上げを行うことになるかもしれない。しかしそれでもなお、国債残高を減らすことは容易ではない。

　しかしながら、2019年度末の政府の金融資産等は約177兆円となっている。したがって、ネットの債務の対GDP比率はおよそ144%となる。この問題を別の視点から観ると、日本銀行は国債を約500兆円保有しているが、これは実質的な国債残高がおよそ500兆円となることを意味している。

　さらに、国債の評価は、民間セクターを含む日本経済の信用力に依存している。日本の対外純資産は約350兆円に上り、また経常収支は長期間巨額の黒字を維持している。外国人投資家が国債を保有している割合は7%程度に過ぎない。これらのデータを総合的に判断すると、私には、日本の財政が必ずしも危機的な状況にあるとは思えない。とはいうものの、インフレはコントロールする必要がある。政府はインフレが加速している間は、国債発行を慎重にすべきであろう。

According to the principle of "System of National Accounts",
$$S - I = G - T$$
S: Savings of private sector; I: Investment of private sector

G: Government expenditure; T: Tax revenue

This equation means; a flow of savings from the private sector $(S-I)$ is equivalent to the volume of fiscal deficit $(G-T)$. The fiscal deficit reflects savings of the private sector, and fiscal reconstruction (fiscal surplus) such as tax hike and expenditure cut, leads to a reduction in savings of the private sector (pressure on livelihoods etc.). An excessive fiscal reconstruction (fiscal surplus) will surely depress the economy. The government needs to strike a balance between economic growth and fiscal reconstruction.

Besides, it can be said that national bonds equal debt for the government, but these are assets for the people. The Ministry of Finance announced in an official statement on their website that any bonds dominated in its own currency from advanced nations such as Japan and the U.S. will never go into default.

UPDATE: Tax revenue in fiscal 2021 increased by 8.5 trillion yen compared to fiscal 2019 despite the depression brought on by the novel coronavirus pandemic. As a consequence, fiscal surplus of the primary balance will be implemented earlier than the Ministry of Finance anticipated. This proves the accuracy of our active fiscal policy. However, the current inflation rate has increased to over 3 %. In order to overcome inflation and reduce the fiscal deficit, it's crucial to raise wages which means an investment in human resources.

Bank of Japan
日本銀行

　国民経済計算の原理によると、S－I＝G－Tの恒等式が成立する。Sは民間セクターの貯蓄。Iは民間セクターの投資。Gは政府支出。Tは税収である。この恒等式が意味するところは、民間セクターの貯蓄の増加（S－I）は、財政赤字の額（G－T）に等しいということである。すなわち、財政赤字は民間セクターの貯蓄を反映しているので、増税や歳出削減などによる財政再建（財政黒字）は、民間セクターの貯蓄の減少（国民生活の圧迫等）につながる。行き過ぎた財政再建は、確実に経済を圧迫するだろう。政府は経済成長と財政再建のバランスをとらなければならない。

　加えて国債は政府にとっては借金ではあるものの、しかし、国民にとっては資産であると言える。財務省はそのホームページで、「日本や米国のような先進国の自国の通貨建ての国債は、債務不履行（デフォルト）に陥ることはありえない」と公式に表明しているのである。

（後日談）

　2021年度の税収は、新型コロナウイルスの世界的大流行による大不況にもかかわらず、2019年度と比べて8.5兆円も増えたのである。その結果、基礎的財政収支（プライマリーバランス）の黒字化は、財務省が予想していたよりも早く達成される見込みとなっている。これは、我々の積極財政政策の正しさを証明している。しかし、最近のインフレ率は3%を超えてきている。インフレを克服して財政赤字を減らすには、人への投資を意味する「賃上げ」が極めて重要となる。

2022年度予算折衝、財務省
Negotiation with the Ministry of
Finance for the 2022 budget, MOF.

Political Debate on the Revision to the Public Prosecutors Office Law
（May 2020）

The ABE Cabinet proposed a revision to the public prosecutors office law in the Diet, resulting in a heated political debate between the ruling bloc and opposition parties. Subsequently, over 6 million critiques and protests have been launched on social media targeting the ABE Cabinet and the ruling coalition.

Under the law in force, Prosecutor General must retire at 65 years of age while prosecutors retire at 63 years of age. This revision bill is as follows. First, to raise the retirement age of prosecutors from 63 to 65. Second, the Deputy Prosecutor General and Superintending prosecutors reaching 63 years of age have to step down to give way to rank-and- file prosecutors. Third, the Prosecutor General who reaches 65 years of age, Deputy Prosecutor General and Superintending Prosecutors 63 years of age are able to continue in their positions for an additional 3 years when the Cabinet deems fit.

The opposition parties protested by arguing that if the revision bill is enacted, the public prosecutors office could be compromised by the Cabinet which would violate the independence of prosecutors and the separation of powers.

For instance, in 1976, the public prosecutors office arrested and indicted former Prime Minister TANAKA Kakuei on suspicion of bribery from Lockheed Corporation. At that time, this was an unprecedented scandal. That is why the opposition insists that this revision to the bill will bend the public prosecutors office through political power.

On the other hand, it is needless to say that the public prosecutors office belongs to the Cabinet. Even in Japan, there have been many

検察庁法改正についての政治的論争
（2020 年 5 月）

　安倍内閣が検察庁法改正案を国会に提出したところ、与野党間の政治的論争が熱気を帯びてきている。その後、600 万を超える批判や抗議が、ソーシャルメディアを通じて安倍内閣や与党に対して発せられているのだ。

　現行の検察庁法では、検事総長は 65 歳で、またその他の検察官は 63 歳で退職しなければならないことになっている。今回の改正案は次の通りだ。すなわち、第 1 に、検察官の退職年齢を 63 歳から 65 歳に引き上げる。第 2 に、63 歳に達した（最高検の）次長検事と高等検察庁の検事長は、役職の無い検事に降格する。第 3 に、65 歳に達した検事総長と、63 歳に達した次長検事と高検の検事長は、内閣が認めた場合には、その地位をさらに（最長）3 年間続けることができるという内容だ。

　野党は論議を通じて、「もしもこの改正案が成立したならば、検察庁は内閣を忖度するようになるかもしれない。このことは検察官の独立と三権分立を侵すことになる」と抗議している。

　たとえば、1976 年、検察庁は元内閣総理大臣であった田中角栄氏を、ロッキード社からの収賄の容疑で逮捕、起訴した。当時、これは前代未聞のスキャンダルであった。それ故野党は、「今回の改正法案は政治権力を通じて検察庁を屈服させるものだ」と主張する。

　その一方で、言うまでもないが、検察庁は内閣に属している。日本においても、これまで多くの冤罪事件があった。たとえば、元厚生労働省事務次官の村木厚子氏は、2009 年に公文書偽造の容疑で逮捕、起訴された。ところが、裁判を通じて、起訴理由となった証拠が、検

reported cases of false accusations. For example, Ms. MURAKI Atsuko, a past administrative vice-Minister of Health, Labour and Welfare, was arrested and indicted on suspicion of forgery of official documents in 2009. However, through the trial, evidence of the indictment turned out to be a fabrication by prosecutors. This was a horrible crime committed by prosecutors.

As a consequence, Ms. MURAKI was found innocent by the court, where on the contrary, the prosecutors in charge of this case were arrested and the Prosecutor General resigned taking responsibility for this incredible crime. Even the public prosecutors office is forbidden to violate human rights.

I think that the purpose of this current revision bill is not to violate the independence of prosecutors or the separation of powers, but instead, to protect human rights by Cabinet control over the public prosecutors office.

However, the ABE Cabinet and the ruling bloc, the LDP and KOMEITO decided to suspend this bill until the extraordinary Diet in fall, taking people's bitter protests into consideration.

Ms. MURAKI Atsuko's interview by KyodoNews, "I felt fear by the falsification of evidence." (Photo: KyodoNews, September 15, 2020) 証拠改ざんは「恐怖感じた」——共同通信社のインタビューに答える村木厚子さん（2020年9月15日、写真＝共同通信社）

察官によって捏造されていたことが明らかになったのだ。これは、検察官による恐ろしい犯罪であった。

その結果、村木氏は裁判所によって無罪が証明されたが、他方で、この事件を担当した検察官たちは逮捕された上に、検事総長はこの信じ難い犯罪の責任をとって辞任したのである。検察庁といえども、人権を侵害することは許されない。

私は、今回の改正法案の目的は、検察官の独立や三権分立を侵すことではなく、むしろ検察庁に対する内閣のコントロールを通じて人権を守ることにあると考えている。

しかしながら、安倍内閣と与党である自民党と公明党は、人々の激しい抗議を考慮して、この法案を秋の臨時国会まで継続審議とすることを決定したのである。

検察庁（東京）
The Public Prosecutors Office, Tokyo.

Coronavirus Creating New Civilizations

(May 2020)

The nature of the coronavirus pandemic knows no bounds. It could be said that human greed created the novel coronavirus, which is considered to live in wild animals. According to the *Economist magazine* in the U.K., China's inland urban development areas have destroyed the natural environment of wild animals, which might have brought on the spread of coronavirus. On the other hand, some media outlets point out that the Chinese government puts an emphasis on traditional Chinese medicines made of herbs or wild animals, adhering to Chinese medicines alongside Western medicines in the fight against the coronavirus pandemic.

Globalism (global economy) has surely accelerated the spread of the novel coronavirus and the world's economies have further deepened mutual dependence on China as the world's factory. Without components made in China, developed countries can't manufacture their products.

Furthermore, Japan imports around 420 million face masks per month from China. They account for 70% of the demand in Japan. The coronavirus pandemic might be a warning against human greed and globalism.

On April 17, the Japanese government declared a second state of emergency for all prefectures, and as a consequence, people had to reduce contact by 80% with others throughout Japan. It should take about one year to develop a coronavirus vaccine and medicines. We must stay at home, work remotely, use online learning and remote medical services for a long period of time, which should nudge us into changing our habits and sense of values.

新型コロナウイルスが新しい文明を創る
（2020 年 5 月）

　新型コロナウイルスの世界的大流行は、留まるところを知らないようだ。人間の欲望が、もともと野生動物の中に生息していたと考えられる新型コロナウイルスを創り出したと言うことができるかもしれない。英国の『エコノミスト』誌によると、「中国内陸部の都市開発が、野生動物の自然環境を破壊しており、このことが新型コロナウイルスの拡散をもたらした」という。その一方で、いくつかのメディアは、「中国政府は植物や野生動物から作られる伝統的な漢方を重視しており、新型コロナウイルスと戦う上で、西洋の薬とともに漢方にこだわっている」と指摘する。

　グローバリズム（グローバル経済）は、確かに新型コロナウイルスの拡散を加速しており、また世界経済は、世界の工場である中国との相互依存を深めている。中国製の部品が無ければ、先進国はその製品を組み立てることができないのである。

　さらに、日本は毎月 4 億 2,000 万枚ものマスクを中国から輸入しているが、それらは日本の需要の 70% を占めている。新型コロナウイルスの世界的大流行は、人間の強欲とグローバリズムに警告を発しているのかもしれない。

　4 月 17 日、日本政府はすべての都道府県に緊急事態宣言を発出したが、その結果、人々は日本中で人との接触を 80% 減らさなければならなくなった。抗ウイルスワクチンや薬を開発するには、約 1 年はかかるだろう。私たちは家にいなければならず、テレワークを行い、オンライン診療や遠隔診療を長い間使わなければならないことになるが、このことは私たちの習慣や価値観の変容を促していくだろう。

People around the world are paying attention to "Social Distancing". In my opinion, there is no denying that civilization has developed through gatherings. For example, religion, festivals, politics, schools, factories and companies. However, "Social Distancing" may reform civilization.

Even if coronavirus vaccines are developed, the human race will still need to continue "Social Distancing". Since the 21st century, we have already faced two dangerous coronaviruses, "SARS" and "MERS". Going forward, unknown viruses will repeatedly emerge and threaten the human race. We can't help transitioning to a "Social Distancing" civilization.

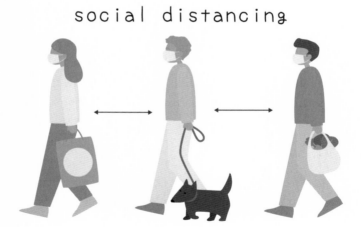

social distancing

　世界中の人々は「ソーシャル・ディスタンス（社会的距離）」に注目している。私の見解であるが、文明というものは人々が集まることで発展してきたことは否定できない。例えば、宗教、祭事、政治、学校、工場、会社などである。しかしながら、「ソーシャル・ディスタンス」は文明を変えるかもしれない。

　たとえ、新型コロナウイルスのワクチンが開発されたとしても、人類は「ソーシャル・ディスタンス」を依然として続ける必要があるだろう。21世紀にはいってからも、人類はすでにSARSやMERSという二つの危険なコロナウイルスと直面してきた。これからも正体の知れないウイルスが繰り返し現れて、人類を脅かすであろう。私たちは、「ソーシャル・ディスタンス」文明に移行していかざるを得ないのである。

Pros and Cons of September Admissions

（June 2020）

As of June 5, 2020, there are over 6.6 million cases of coronavirus and nearly 400,000 fatalities around the world. One of the most crucial agendas Japan faces at the moment is how to guarantee education from elementary school to university amid the coronavirus pandemic.

In Japan, many prefectural governors proposed a "September Admission" in order to solve this issue, and Prime Minister ABE promised to discuss this issue with his cabinet as soon as possible.

Proponents consider the merits of a "September Admission" as follows: First, students could recover the delays in learnings attributed to the coronavirus pandemic. Second, it would be easier for Japanese students to study overseas and for foreigners to enroll in Japanese universities. Thirdly, Japanese students would be able to avoid entrance examinations amid influenza season in winter.

On the other hand, opponents point out that a "September Admission" would generate an enormous negative influence to our society such as a change in the fiscal year, recruitment by corporations, a postponement of entrance examinations, a delay of school age, an increase of students in the same grade, and so on.

The ABE Cabinet is slated to show its agenda in early June and decide on the direction for this matter. However, if a "September Admission" started during another wave of the novel coronavirus, what should we do? Society would be forced to close all our schools again. It would all be in vain.

If a "September Admission" started, would Japanese students who want to study overseas or foreigners who want to study in Japan really increase?

9月入学は是か非か

（2020 年 6 月）

　2020 年 6 月 5 日現在、世界の新型コロナウイルスの患者数は 660 万人を超えており、死者数も 40 万人に近づいている。目下日本が直面する最も重要な課題のひとつは、新型コロナウイルスの世界的大流行の中で、いかにして小学校から大学までの教育を保証するかである。

　日本では、多くの都道府県知事たちがこの問題を解決するために、「9 月入学」を提唱している。これを受けて、安倍首相はできるだけ早期に内閣で検討することを約束した。

　「9 月入学」賛成派は、「9 月入学」の利点を次のように考えている。すなわち、第 1 に、生徒たちは新型コロナウイルスの世界的大流行による学習の遅れを、「9 月入学」によって取り戻すことができること。第 2 に、日本の学生が海外留学をする場合や、外国人が日本の大学に入学する時に、（海外は 9 月入学が多いので）スムーズになるというもの。第 3 に、日本の生徒たちがインフルエンザの季節に試験を受けることを避けられることである。

　その一方で、反対派は、「9 月入学」が社会に大変大きなマイナスの影響を産み出すことを指摘する。例えば、会計年度の変更、企業の採用活動、入学試験の延期、就学年齢の遅れ、同一学年の生徒の増加などである。

　安倍内閣は 6 月の初めには、（9 月入学のための）課題を提示し、この問題に対する方向性を決定するとしている。しかしながら、もしも「9 月入学」がスタートした時に、新型コロナウイルスの次の波が襲ってきたら、どうするのか。社会は再びすべての学校の閉鎖を余儀なくされるだろう。それではすべてが無駄になる。

In order to implement a "September Admission", Japanese society will need to make tremendous efforts. I don't think that the pros of a "September Admission" surpasses the cons.

On May 26, the state of emergency was lifted and all schools and universities were closed for two months. However, I suppose that most students will be able to recover from the delays in learning by making effective use of summer and winter vacations.

The most crucial point is to guarantee a safe environment for education. Therefore, all schools and universities have to practice social distancing, and avoid the 3Cs: crowded spaces without ventilation, crowded conditions and conversations within close proximity. Teachers need to create a "New Normal" for education by utilizing online classes. It seems to me that the idea of a "September Admission" itself has already become outdated.

UPDATE: The ruling coalition, the LDP and KOMEITO requested the government to suspend an introduction of a "September Admission" in 2021, and as a consequence, Prime Minister ABE agreed it upon.

Kyoto University
京都大学

　もしも、「９月入学」が始まれば、海外留学したい日本の生徒や、日本で学びたい外国人が本当に増えるだろうか。

　「９月入学」を実現するためには、社会はとてつもない努力を必要とするだろう。私には「９月入学」の利点が欠点を上回るとは思えない。

　５月26日に「緊急事態」が解除された。すべての学校と大学は２か月間閉鎖されていた。しかしながら、ほとんどの生徒たちは、夏休みと冬休みを効果的に使うことで、学習の遅れを取り戻すことができるだろう。

　最も重要な点は、安全な教育環境を保証することである。したがって、すべての学校と大学は「ソーシャル・ディスタンス」を実践し、３密を避けなければならない。すなわち、３密とは、空調設備の無い密閉空間、密集状態、そして密接な会話である。教師は、オンライン授業を利用することで、教育の「新常態（ニューノーマル）」を作り出す必要がある。私には、「９月入学」のアイデアは、それ自体もはや時代遅れになっているように思えるのだ。

（後日談）

　後日、連立与党の自民党と公明党は、2021年の「９月入学」の導入の停止を政府に申し入れたところ、安倍首相はそれに同意したのである。

桜、同志社大学（京都）
Cherry blossoms, Doshisha
University, Kyoto.

China's Grave Decision on National Security in Hong Kong
(June 2020)

On May 22, 2020, the National People's Congress of China (NPC), which was postponed for two months due to the coronavirus epidemic, made a crucial decision regarding national security for Hong Kong. The major point of this decision is that the NPC authorized its standing committee to enact new legislation to prevent serious damage to national security in Hong Kong and ban foreign powers from meddling in the governance of Hong Kong. Those who violate this new law will be punished.

Hong Kong had been a territory of China since ancient times; however, it was occupied by the U.K. after the Opium War in the 1840's. On December 19, 1984, the U.K. and China signed a joint communique regarding Hong Kong issues and confirmed the recovery of China's sovereignty over Hong Kong from July 1, 1997.

Based on this communique, the Basic Law for the Hong Kong Special Administrative Region (Basic Law) was enacted, which described the "One Country, Two Systems", which stated a high degree of autonomy, legislative power, independence of jurisdiction, preservation of capitalism for 50 years, the right to private property and so on.

Specifically, article 23 of the Basic Law describes that the Hong Kong Special Administrative Region must enact legislation on national security on its own accord. However, it hasn't been implemented until now.

In 2003, the Hong Kong government tried to propose legislation in accordance with the Basic Law, but this resulted in its withdrawal due to huge demonstrations of around 500,000 people. Last year, protests surrounding the extradition bill expanded into

香港の国家安全に関する中国の重大決定

（2020 年 6 月）

　新型コロナウイルスの流行のために 2 カ月間延期されていた中国の全国人民代表大会（全人代）は、5 月 22 日、香港の国家安全に関する重大な決定を行った。この決定の主要なポイントは、香港の国家安全に対する深刻な損害を防ぎ、外国勢力が香港の統治に介入することを禁止するため、全人代が常務委員会に対して新たな法律の制定を授権したことである。この新法に違反するものは、罰せられることになるだろう。

　香港は古代から中国の領土であったが、1840 年代のアヘン戦争の後、大英帝国に占領された。1984 年 12 月 19 日、英国と中国は香港問題に関する共同声明に調印し、1997 年 7 月 1 日から、香港に対する中国の主権が回復することを確認した。

　この共同声明をもとに、香港特別行政区基本法（香港基本法）が制定された。その中で「一国二制度」を規定し、高度の自治、立法権、司法の独立、50 年間資本主義を維持すること、私有財産制度などについて述べている。

　とりわけ、香港基本法の 23 条は、「香港特別行政区は自主的に国家安全に関する法律を制定しなければならない」と規定している。しかしながら、それは今に至るまで実現していない。

　2003 年、香港政庁は香港基本法にしたがって（新たな国家安全に関する）法律を提案しようとしたが、これは約 50 万人もの巨大なデモによって撤回に至った。また 2019 年は、逃亡犯条例をめぐる抗議が大規模なデモに拡大し、多くの破壊行為を引き起こした。

　その結果、中国政府は、香港政庁が独自に国家安全法を制定するこ

large scale demonstrations, raising a storm of riots.

As a consequence, the Chinese government found it difficult for the Hong Kong government to enact National Security legislation on its own. However, given article 23 of the Basic Law regarding national security in Hong Kong, this decision of the NPC is thought to be a denial of the "One Country, Two Systems" agreement.

U.S. president Donald Trump announced various sanctions against China due to the reinforcement of China's control on Hong Kong leading to a façade of the "One Country, Two Systems" policy. The Chinese government raised strong objection to Trump's firm stance, saying that "Issues over Hong Kong are internal affairs. Trump's sanctions are ridiculous, and we will take countermeasures against U.S. sanctions".

I am seriously concerned that the high degree of autonomy and fundamental human rights in Hong Kong may be gutted by the decision of the NPC. The "One Country, Two Systems" agreement must be strictly protected, since it is guaranteed by the Basic Law.

Hong Kong

とは困難であると判断した。しかしながら、香港の国家安全に関する基本法 23 条を考慮すると、今回の全人代の決定は「一国二制度」を否定することになると考えられる。

　米国のドナルド・トランプ大統領は、「一国二制度」の形骸化につながる、中国の香港に対する統制の強化を理由として、様々な制裁を中国に課すと発表した。中国政府は、「香港をめぐる問題は内政問題である。トランプ大統領の制裁は馬鹿げており、我々は米国の制裁に対して対抗手段を取ることになるだろう」と述べ、トランプ大統領の強硬な姿勢に強く反発した。

　私は、香港の高度の自治や基本的人権は、全人代の決定によって骨抜きになるかもしれないと大変懸念している。「一国二制度」の合意は厳格に守られなければならない。それは香港基本法に保証されているからである。

香港の独立を訴える大規模デモ（2019 年）
Large scale demonstrations, Hong Kong, 2019.

"Black Lives Matter" in America

（June 2020）

On May 25, 2020, a black man named George Floyd died after a white police officer pressed his knee into Floyd's neck for 8 minutes and 46 seconds as he was facedown on the ground, unarmed and handcuffed in Minneapolis. "Please, please I can't breathe". Floyd's voice went viral on social media around the world. Police described Floyd as a suspect of forgery at a grocery store, where the clerk called police after he apparently used counterfeit money to buy cigarettes. However, this response by police was excessive. Four police officers were fired over the incident, and one of them was arrested and charged with murder.

This incident galvanized massive protests and accusations of systemic racism in America, with some protesters rioting and looting. U.S. President Trump requested the U.S. military police units be ready to deploy to Minneapolis and he called the protesters "Thugs" in a tweet, saying "When the looting starts, the shooting starts". His tweet fanned flames of hate. Moreover, the president demanded the nation's governors on the phone to dominate protesters, accusing some of them of being weak.

On the other hand, Secretary Mark Esper publicly opposed using active duty troops against American citizens, saying that the option to use active duty forces in a law enforcement role should only be used as a matter of last resort.

The efforts of many communities in the U.S. to acknowledge the pain began to bridge the divide. For instance, police officers were kneeling with protesters during a rally, saying "We will protect you, we will march with you".

Nevertheless, protests didn't settle. The demonstrations have

米国の「黒人の命の問題」
（2020 年 6 月）

　2020 年 5 月 25 日、ミネアポリスで、警察官がジョージ・フロイドという黒人を地面に押し倒し、手錠をかけ、8 分 46 秒もの間、無抵抗の黒人の首を上から膝で抑えつけた結果、その黒人は死亡した。「お願いだ。息ができない」というフロイドの声は、その（悲惨な）映像とともに瞬く間に世界中に拡散された。警察は、フロイドが食料品店でタバコを買うのに明らかに偽札を使った後、店員が警察に通報したので、偽造通貨使用罪の容疑者としている。しかしながら、この警察の反応は行き過ぎであった。4 人の警察官は解雇された上に、その 1 人は逮捕され殺人罪で起訴された。

　この事件は大きな抗議とともに、米国における根深い人種差別に対する告発に火をつけ、ある者たちは暴動や略奪まで行った。トランプ大統領は、米軍にミネアポリスへ展開する準備を要請した上に、ツイートでこれらの抗議者を「ならず者」と呼び、「もしも略奪が始まった時には、銃撃が始まる」と脅かしたのである。しかも大統領は、知事たちに電話で「抗議者たちを制圧せよ」と要求し、ある知事たちを「弱腰だ」と責めたのである。

　その一方で、エスパー国防長官は公式に、米国民に対して軍を向けることに反対し、「治安維持のために軍を使うという選択肢は、最後の手段に限られるべきだ」と述べている。

　米国の多くのコミュニティで人々の痛みを知ろうとする努力が、国民の分断に橋を架け始めている。例えば、警察官たちは、集会の間、抗議者たちとともに膝を地面について、「我々はあなたたちを守る。我々はあなたたちとともに行進する」と語っている。

further expanded across the U.S. and around the world, despite fears of coronavirus infection. Even in Osaka, Japan, about one thousand protesters demonstrated on the street chanting "Black Lives Matter".

The former vice president, Biden said "The country is crying out for leadership. Leadership that can recognize pain and deep grief of communities". President Trump should have expressed his sincere condolences for the loss of George Floyd. He should have showed his resolution not to repeat such a brutal crime attributed to racism.

On the other side of the world, China said that the U.S. is ineligible to criticize China for issues in Hong Kong. I hope a new wave for human rights will emerge in the U.S.A. and throughout the world.

　それにもかかわらず、抗議は収まらない。デモは、コロナウイルスの感染の恐れがあるにもかかわらず、米国中に、また世界中に拡大している。日本の大阪市でも、約 1,000 人の抗議者たちが "Black Lives Matter" と叫びながらデモを行った。

　前副大統領のバイデン氏は、「この国はリーダーシップを求めている。人々の痛みとコミュニティの深い悲しみを知ることのできるリーダーシップを」と述べた。トランプ大統領は、ジョージ・フロイド氏の死に対して、深い哀悼の意を表すべきであった。また、人種差別に起因するこのような残虐な犯罪を 2 度と繰り返さないという決意を示すべきであったのだ。

　世界では一方で、中国は、「米国は香港問題で中国を批判する資格はない」と述べている。私は、新しい人権の波が米国で、また世界中で起こってくることを期待している。

Attitudes amid the Pandemic
(July 2020)

As of June 30, the number of confirmed coronavirus cases has topped 10 million, with a death toll near 500,000 around the world. This pandemic has become the worst infectious catastrophe since the Spanish influenza (1918-1920). Under such a calamity, people tend to reveal their true nature.

Due to the state of emergency, the Japanese economy has plummeted.

Specifically, small and medium-sized companies are suffering from sharp declines in sales, and many employees have lost their jobs or are forced to accept a cut in their wages. Some people are full of frustration and complaints, and as a consequence, they have launched attacks on politicians, especially Diet members. For example, people frequently insist that annual allowances for Diet members should be cut, since they don't understand people's sufferings. However, many people aren't aware that these annual allowances have already been reduced by 20%.

Furthermore, it's a problem that domestic violence and various forms of harassment have increased due to stresses and strains.

The government has doled out ¥100,000 per person and provided ¥2 million for small companies that declined in sales more than 50% compared to the previous year. Nevertheless, some people require further provisions, saying that the benefits from the government are insufficient.

On social media platforms such as Twitter, there are both agreements and insults against my opinions, for instance, anonymously saying "How foolish you are! Are you really a Diet member? ".

パンデミック下の人々の振る舞い
（2020 年 7 月）

　6 月 30 日現在、世界中で確認されている新型コロナウイルスの感染者数は、1,000 万人を超え、死者数も 50 万人に近づいている。このパンデミックは、1918 年から 1920 年に世界的に流行したスペイン風邪以来、最悪の感染症の大災害となっている。このような惨事のもとでは、人々はその本性がむき出しになる傾向がある。

　非常事態宣言が発令されたため、日本経済は急速に悪化している。とりわけ、中小企業は売り上げの激減に苦しんでおり、多くの従業員はその職を失い、あるいは賃金のカットを受け入れることを余儀なくされている。人々はフラストレーションや不満に満ちており、その結果、政治家、特に国会議員に攻撃を向ける者もいる。例えば、「国会議員は人々の苦しみを理解していないから、国会議員の歳費を削減すべきだ」という主張がしばしばなされる。しかし、多くの人々は、国会議員の歳費がすでに 20% 減額されていることを知らないのである。

　さらには、ストレスや緊張から、ドメスティック・バイオレンス（DV）や様々な形でのハラスメントが増加していることは問題である。

　政府は国民一人当たりに 10 万円を支給し始めており、また前年度と比べて 50% 以上売り上げが落ちている中小企業には 200 万円を給付しているところだ。それにもかかわらず、一部の人々は「政府からの給付は不十分だ」と言って、さらなる給付を要求している。

　ツイッターなどのソーシャルメディアでは、私の意見に対して賛成だけではなく、侮辱的な投稿もなされている。例えば、匿名で「あなたは何と愚かなのだ。あなたは本当に国会議員なのか」などである。

　その一方で、思慮深い人々もいる。新型コロナウイルスの感染の初

On the other hand, there are some of consideration. In the beginning, the biggest problem our society faced was shortage of face masks, where no one could purchase them anywhere. So, several small companies gradually began to produce face masks to those who were troubled by this shortage.

In most hospitals, medical staff were facing severe shortages of personal protective equipment (PPE) such as surgical masks, N95 masks, gowns and face shields, despite the government's utmost efforts to provide these goods. It has also been reported that people presented hand-made gowns or face shields to hospitals in need.

Under such a crisis, we can clearly see the contrast between the discourteous and the charitable. At any rate, Diet members have no choice but to accept the reality and contradiction as they are.

期の頃は、我々の社会が直面した最大の課題はマスクの不足であったが、しかし、誰もどこへ行ってもマスクを買うことができなかった。そこで、いくつかの小さな会社が、マスクが無くて困っている人々のためにマスクを作り始めたのだった。

　ほとんどの病院では、医療従事者は、サージカルマスク、N95 マスク、ガウン、フェイスシールドなどの防護装備（PPE）の厳しい不足に直面していた。政府は、最大限の供給努力をしていたにもかかわらずである。そのため、市民たちが自分たちでガウンやフェイスシールドを作って、必要とする病院に届けたりしてくれているのである。

　このような危機のもとでは、ぶしつけな態度と、他方で思いやりのある行動の対比を鮮やかに見て取ることができる。いずれにしても、国会議員は、現実とその矛盾をありのままに受け入れるより他はないのである。

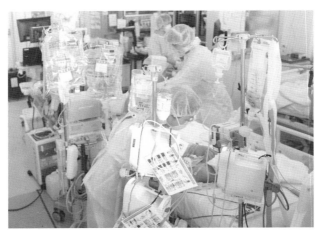

聖マリアンナ医科大学病院の集中治療室（ICU）で、新型コロナウイルスの重症患者の治療に当たる医療従事者（2020年4月、川崎市、写真＝共同通信社）
The ICU of St. Marianna University Hospital. Medical staff treating seriously ill patients with COVID-19. (Kawasaki City, Photo: KyodoNews, April, 2020)

The Liberal Democratic Party (LDP)
—What traits are needed to be Prime Minister?
(August 2020)

It has been over 20 years since the LDP and the KOMEITO ruling coalition began in 1999. The LDP has consistently been the ruling bloc since the merger of two conservative parties in 1955, save for the Hosokawa administration (1993-1994), and the Democratic Party of Japan (DPJ) administration (2009-2012). Currently, the LDP accounts for the majority in both Houses (283/465, House of Representatives; 122/242, House of Councillors).

It is said that the LDP Diet members chiefly consist of those who are second-generation law makers, past bureaucrats, landowners, medium and small business managers, local assembly members, representatives from industrial communities, and so on. Prime Minister ABE himself is a typical second-generation Diet member.

Members have to create their own campaign clubs to gain votes and funds for elections. Second-generation candidates will usually inherit their parent's campaign clubs, which of course is advantageous for a successful election in their constituencies.

Furthermore, past bureaucrat Diet members are in general excellent in their ability for policy making; however, they usually need strong backings to climb the ladder of success in the political world. Roughly speaking, second-generation Diet members are affluent.

In the LDP, many Diet members belong to a faction and play various roles within that faction and colleagues. By winning multiple elections, they earn trust of their seniors and colleagues. Generally speaking, a member who has been elected at least six times is recommended as a first time minister by their superiors.

In order to become head of a faction, they have to be a person of character with power to maintain the faction.

Secretary-General of the LDP, Chief Cabinet Secretary, and the Finance Minister are very important positions and gateways to become a future prime minister. Among these VIPs which includes leaders of factions, the LDP President is elected by Diet members and local party members of these networks. Subsequently, this candidate will be approved as the Prime Minister in the House of Representatives.

Charisma is an important factor for a Prime Minister. In Japan, many Prime Ministers have been second-generation Diet members. They need this charisma to make people believe.

Mr. ASO Taro, the current Minister of Finance, is a past Prime Minister (2008-2009) and the grandchild to Mr. YOSHIDA Shigeru who was a popular Prime Minister (1948-1954). Mr. KISHIDA Fumio, the Chairperson of the Policy Affairs Research Council of the LDP, is regarded as a candidate for the next Prime Minister. Mr. ISHIBA Shigeru, the leader of the ISHIBA faction, is a powerful rival to Prime Minister ABE. Both of these men are also second-generation Diet members. Mr. KOIZUMI Shinjiro is a promising young politician and the son of the past Prime Minister KOIZUMI Junichiro, who was also a second-generation Diet member.

In the LDP, hereditary Diet members make up over 30%, which is higher than other parties. Media outlets regularly criticize the hereditary system as an invisible barrier for people who want to become politicians. However, some hereditary Diet members have qualities and capabilities needed to be political leaders. For example, charisma has nothing to do with academic backgrounds. Nevertheless, charisma including passion, courage, perseverance, responsibility, judgement, and a broad-minded character are crucial traits for a Prime Minister.

The KOMEITO Party
—Against the Devil of Power
(August 2020)

The KOMEITO was established based on the SOKA GAKKAI (SG), a religious organization in 1964, and at that time, the LDP was a one-party administration. The LDP chiefly reflected the profits of capitalists while the largest opposition party, the Social Democratic Party (SDP) was based on labor unions. In those days, however, there were many people who belonged to neither the capitalist class nor to labor unions. They were so called "The Masses" and the KOMEITO was able to absorb these people. As of 2020, the KOMEITO, a member of the ruling coalition with the LDP, has 57 Diet members (29 in the House of Representatives, 38 in the House of Councillors).

Based on this history, Diet members of the KOMEITO have been selected from various classes such as lawyers, bureaucrats, businessmen of big enterprises or banks, medical doctors, certified accountants, local assembly members, journalist, teacher, artist and so on. However, there are very few managers of small and medium-sized companies, or large landowners. It can be said that KOMEITO members mostly belong to the middle class.

The philosophy of the KOMEITO is based on humanism and pacifism, and its political consciousness is centrist including center right and left. Therefore, opinions of the KOMEITO reflect an average way of thinking for Japanese people, which is very helpful for the LDP when making decisions. The KOMEITO plays a key role in stabilizing the ABE administration, and preventing the LDP from getting out of hand.

The Minister of Land, Infrastructure, Transport and Tourism

has been a designated seat for the KOMEITO since 2004, except during the DPJ administration (2009-2012). However, given the power of the KOMEITO, the LDP should transfer one more minister posting to the KOMEITO. Though, the KOMEITO is not so greedy as to require another post.

The KOMEITO Diet members are on the whole considered humane, ethical and clean. Specifically, ethics is a prerequisite trait for a politician. Innumerable politicians have lost their positions due to ethical scandals such as bribery, violations of the Public Offices Election Law, illicit relationships, power harassment, gaffes and so on. This is true for every party and politician, including the KOMEITO. It is no exaggeration to say that politicians must be careful with "The Devil of Power" which tempts them to commit sins. Without a solid bedrock of ethics, any politician could easily surrender to "The Devil of Power".

The KOMEITO is firmly supported by the SG. However, I suppose that all the KOMEITO parliamentary members, both Diet and local assemblies, need to create their own campaign clubs to further extend the party's strength.

The KOMEITO
Headquarters, Tokyo.
公明党本部（東京）

The Opposition Parties

(August 2020)

At present, the main opposition parties in the Diet consist of the Constitutional Democratic Party of Japan (CDP), the Democratic Party (DP), the Japan Innovation Party (JIP), the Social Democratic Party (SDP), and the Japanese Communist Party (JCP).

The distribution of power in both Houses are as follows; all the opposition parties and independents hold 253 seats (Main opposition; CDP 90, DP 60, JIP 25, SDP 4, JCP 25), while the ruling bloc hold the majority at 455 seats (LDP 398, KOMEITO 57).

The CDP and DP are products of schism of the now defunct Democratic Party of Japan (DPJ). It can be said that the CDP is center left while the DP is centrist, both parties are backed by labor unions. However, I heard that some members of these parties first desired to enter the LDP, but were rejected due to competition with LDP candidates running in the same constituencies. Many Diet members from these parties experienced the DPJ administration (2009-2012) and have survived until today.

The JIP is a conservative party based in Osaka prefecture, insisting on drastic administrative restoration. Most members of the JIP shifted from the LDP. The JIP has been known to seek a collaboration with the LDP regarding the Constitutional amendment issue, and with the KOMEITO in terms of the new Osaka Metropolitan plan.

Since the ABE administration led by the LDP-KOMEITO ruling coalition has continued for 7 years, the opposition parties, with exception of the JIP, are trying to cooperate with each other in the next general election.

However, it has been very difficult for the CDP and DP to cooperate with the Japanese Communist Party (JCP) due to the vast differences in their political principles and policies. In particular, the Japanese Trade Union Confederation which supports the CDP and the DP, disapproves of a JCP tie up for the next general election.

The causes of the DPJ administration's failure were stated in my earlier book entitled *Japanese Politics; One Politician's Perspective / From the DPJ administration to the LDP-KOMEITO ruling coalition (2010-2019)*. Each Diet member from each opposition party is excellent in their ability for policy making due to their academic backgrounds or careers. However, in order to get back power, they first have to create a new administration plan based on firm principles and policies to compete with the LDP-KOMEITO ruling coalition. Subsequently, they need to overcome many issues such as party governance, how to deal with bureaucrats, and how to coordinate with other parties.

Conference by opposition party leaders. (The Diet, Photo: KyodoNews, July 30, 2020)
野党党首会談に臨む面々、国会要求で一致（2020 年 7 月 30 日、国会、写真＝共同通信社）

General Election or Cabinet Resignation?
(August 2020)

Mr. ABE Shinzo has become the longest serving Prime Minister in Japan from August 24, surpassing past Prime Minister SATO Eisaku, ABE's great uncle, with a consecutive tenure in office of 2,798 days, and counting. He is also the president of the Liberal Democratic Party (LDP), and his term doesn't expire until September 2021. A revision of the LDP's rule that describes 3 terms and 9 years for the presidency would be needed for him to continue his leadership.

Furthermore, the current term for the present members of the House of Representatives is due to expire in October 2021. Therefore, the focal point is when Prime Minister ABE will dissolve the House of Representatives, or when will he resign before his term expires and if so; who will succeed him?

However, it seems to me that Prime Minister ABE is tired due to his long tenure and has no intention to further extend his term. I find it difficult to believe that Mr. ABE will achieve a Constitutional amendment in terms of Article 9.

As of August 13, 2020, the number of the novel coronavirus infections exceeded 20 million around the world, with a death toll over 744,000. In Japan, there are near 52,600 confirmed cases and over 1,000 fatalities. It looks like a second wave of the coronavirus epidemic is surging across the nation. Under such severe conditions, a general election would be difficult.

Moreover, we have to take it into consideration whether the Tokyo Olympic and Paralympic games can really be held in July 2021. It has been reported that the International Olympic Committee (IOC) will make this decision in October 2020.

解散か、それとも内閣総辞職か

（2020 年 8 月）

　安倍晋三氏は 8 月 24 日、彼の大叔父である佐藤栄作元総理の連続 2,798 日の在任期間を超えて、日本で最も長い在任期間の首相となったが、なおそれを更新し続けている。彼はまた自由民主党の総裁でもあり、その任期は 2021 年の 9 月までとなっている。彼が総裁を続けるためには、総裁の任期を 3 期 9 年と規定している自民党の規約を改定することが必要であろう。

　さらには、現在の衆議院議員の任期は、2021 年 10 月に切れることになっている。したがって、焦点は、安倍首相がいつ衆議院を解散するのか、あるいは、任期が来る前にいつ辞職するのか、その場合は誰が後を継ぐのか、ということになる。

　しかしながら、私には、安倍首相は長い在任期間の故に疲れており、その任期をさらに延長するつもりはないように見える。安倍首相が憲法 9 条の改正を実現することは困難であると観ている。

　2020 年の 8 月 13 日の時点で、新型コロナウイルスの感染者数は世界中で 2,000 万人を超えており、死者数は 74 万 4,000 人となっている。日本では、約 5 万 2,600 人の感染者が確認されており、1,000 人以上が亡くなっている。コロナウイルスの第 2 波の流行が国中を襲っているようだ。このような厳しい状況のもとでは、衆議院総選挙は難しいであろう。

　しかも、東京オリンピック・パラリンピックが、本当に 2021 年 7 月に開催できるかどうかも考慮に入れなければならない。国際オリンピック委員会はこの決断を 2020 年 10 月にするだろうと報道されている。米国のドナルド・トランプ大統領が再選されるかどうかも、安

Whether U.S. President Donald Trump can be reelected is another important factor that will affect Prime Minister ABE.

In June 2021, the Tokyo Metropolitan Parliamentary election is slated to be held. The KOMEITO attaches great importance to the Tokyo Metropolitan Parliamentary elections, and doesn't desire a general election at that time. Therefore, whoever the Prime Minister is, the chance for a general election is restricted.

Mr. KISHIDA, chairperson of the Policy Research Council of the LDP, Mr. ISHIBA, past Secretary-General of the LDP, and Mr. SUGA, the Chief Cabinet Secretary are all slated to be potential successors to Prime Minister ABE. Political tactics between these three factions has already begun.

UPDATE: On August 28, Prime Minister ABE Shinzo abruptly announced that he will resign due to his intractable disease regarding large intestine. In his first administration (2006-2007), he had a difficult decision to step down due to the same disease. The LDP is slated to hold an election campaign for the presidency from September 8 to 15, and a new Prime Minister will be nominated on September 16 in the Diet.

The Prime Minister's Office, Tokyo.
首相官邸（東京）

倍首相に影響を与える重要な要因である。

　2021 年 6 月には、東京都議会議員選挙が予定されている。公明党は、この都議会議員選挙を大変重要視しており、衆議院総選挙との同時選挙は望んでいない。したがって、誰が首相であろうとも、総選挙のチャンスは限られている。

　自由民主党の政務調査会長の岸田氏、元自民党幹事長の石破 茂 氏、そして現官房長官の菅氏らが、安倍首相の後継者であると見做されている。これら 3 つの派閥の間での駆け引きは、すでに始まっているのだ。

（後日談）

　8 月 28 日、安倍晋三首相は突如、大腸の難病を理由として辞任することを発表した。第 1 次安倍政権（2006 ～ 2007）でも、同じ病気のために辞任するという辛い決断をしている。自民党は、9 月 8 日から 15 日の間で総裁選挙を行うことを予定しており、その結果、9 月 16 日には国会で新首相が指名されることになる。

公明党青年局が菅首相に提言
The KOMEITO's youth division submitted a proposal to Prime Minister SUGA.

Mr. SUGA Yoshihide becomes the 99th Prime Minister of Japan
(September 2020)

On September 16, 2020, Mr. SUGA Yoshihide, Chief Cabinet Secretary of the ABE Cabinet, was elected as the 99th Prime Minister of Japan. This is the first time that a Chief Cabinet Secretary was elected to the office of Prime Minister due to the resignation of an incumbent Prime Minister. He is the first politician to assume the office of Prime Minister without belonging to any faction.

According to his book, Mr. SUGA was born in 1948, as the third of four children to a strawberry farmer in a remote village of Akita Prefecture in northern Japan. After graduating high school, he headed to the capital Tokyo and worked for a factory. However, two months later he resigned, and began preparing for entrance exams for university while taking side jobs at the Tsukiji market early in the morning in order to save money for university.

Two years later, Mr. SUGA entered Hosei University, the Department of Politics faculty of law, due to the lower tuition fees among private universities in Tokyo. While in university, he worked part-time as a security guard at the NHK, at a newspaper company and at a curry store to cover his tuition fees and household expenses.

During university, Mr. SUGA belonged to the Karate club for four years and earned the rank of 3rd Dan. In 1973, he graduated from university and got a job with a private company.

However, Mr. SUGA was determined to become a politician, since he fully realized that politics changes society. In 1975, at 26, he landed a job as a secretary to OKONOGI Hikoshiro, a member of the House of Representatives from Yokohama. In 1987, he challenged to run for the Yokohama City assembly election while visiting 30,000 houses and wearing out six pairs of shoes, which resulted in his remarkable victory.

In 1996, Mr. SUGA was first elected as a member of the House of Representatives from the second single-seat constituency of Kanagawa prefecture. After taking office as the parliamentary secretary of Land, Infrastructure, Transport and Tourism, and as vice Minister of Internal Affairs and Communications, he was appointed as the Minister of Internal Affairs and Communications during the first ABE Cabinet in 2006. In 2012, he was appointed as the Chief Cabinet Secretary during the second ABE administration and had continued this post for seven years and eight months, until September 2020.

I highly value Mr. SUGA as a statesman of indomitable spirit. He started with nothing and worked his way up to Prime Minister. He is the first Prime Minister to work as a municipality assembly member. Therefore, he knows well what people really need.

Currently, Mr. SUGA has pledged the inception of a "Digital Agency" which will proceed with the digitalization of government, the addition of health insurance for fertility treatment, drastic reforms for compartmentalized administrative structure, and the reduction of cellar phone' fees.

These are why expectations for the new Prime Minister are rising, and as a consequence, the approval rate for the SUGA Cabinet has reached 74%, which is higher than the second ABE Cabinet in 2012.

The KOMEITO has a firm relationship with Prime Minister SUGA. In 2015, the KOMEITO insisted on the introduction of a reduced consumption tax rate for foods, while the LDP and the Ministry of Finance (MOF) opposed it. At that time, Chief Cabinet Secretary SUGA intervened and persuaded the LDP to accept the request of the KOMEITO.

My new role as the Chairperson of the Policy Research Council of the KOMEITO

(January 2021)

On September 27, 2020, I was appointed Chairperson of the Policy Research Council (CPRC) of the KOMEITO. It was like a bolt from the blue to me and most Diet members of the KOMEITO.

The CPRC is one of the most important posts. The three top-ranking officials of the KOMEITO consists of Chief Representative, Secretary-General and CPRC.

I suppose the CPRC is also one of the busiest posts for the KOMEITO. Many people, such as bureaucrats and private citizens, visit my office one after another every day, and I also attend various conferences of industrial associations regarding budgets and taxes. I play a central role in the decision of personnel matters for the Policy Research Council and formulate major policies of the KOMEITO which needs to be discussed on the Committee of Standing Directors. It's hard work to make decisions while considering the various opinions among directors.

Moreover, I deliberate as a representative of the KOMEITO in the Budget Committee, and hold press briefings every Wednesday where I am requested to answer any questions from political correspondents. Furthermore, I often participate in debate programs on TV.

In November 2020, following the EU and the U.S., a third wave of novel coronavirus infections has been surging in Japan. Prime Minister SUGA ordered the government to formulate additional economic policy packages in order to curtail the spread of infections, and prompt reform of private companies, leading to good economic circulation. I immediately led the Policy Research Council to formulate additional economic policy packages including

公明党の政務調査会長に就任

（2021 年 1 月）

　2020 年 9 月 27 日、私は公明党の政務調査会長を拝命した。それは私にとって、まさに青天の霹靂であった。公明党のほとんどの国会議員にとっても同様であろう。

　政務調査会長は最も重要なポストの一つであり、公明党では代表、幹事長とともに三役と呼ばれている。

　私は、政務調査会長は公明党の中で、最も忙しいポストの一つであると思う。官僚や民間人など多くの方々が、毎日次から次へと私の事務所を訪れる上に、私自身も、予算や税制に関して様々な業界団体の会合に出席する。また、政務調査会の人事や、公明党の主要な政策を決定する上で、私が中心的な役割を果たしているが、それらは党の常任役員会でも議論する必要がある。役員間の様々な意見を考慮して意思決定することは、なかなかのハードワークである。

　さらに、私は公明党を代表して予算委員会で質問を行い、また毎週水曜日には記者会見を行うことになっている。そこでは、（マスコミ各社の）政治部記者からの、あらゆる質問に答えることが求められている。加えて、テレビ討論会にもしばしば出演する。

　2020 年の 11 月には、EU や米国に続いて、日本でも新型コロナウイルス感染の第 3 波が襲ってきた。そこで菅首相は、政府に感染拡大を抑えるとともに、民間企業の改革を促し、経済の好循環につなげるため、追加の経済対策を編成するように命じた。私は直ちに政務調査会を率いて、防災減災対策を含む追加の経済政策の策定にとりかかり、11 月 24 日に菅首相に提出した。

　同時に、2021 年度予算編成は最終局面を迎えていた。しかしなが

disaster prevention, which I proposed to Prime Minister SUGA on November 24.

At the same time, the 2021 budget compilation reached its closing stages; however, there were several problems. One of these was the out-of-pocket medical expenses for the elderly aged 75 and over which is currently at 10% as a general rule. Prime Minister SUGA planned to establish a new 20% burden, aiming to reduce insurance premiums for the working-age generation.

However, I insisted to postpone an increase due to the spread of the novel coronavirus, and to restrict 20% burden to those who have a sufficient annual income, such as 2.4 million yen or more in a single-person household.

Nevertheless, Prime Minister SUGA firmly ordered Mr. SHIMOMURA, the Chairperson of the Policy Research Council of the LDP and Mr. TAMURA, the Minister of Health, Labour and Welfare to persuade me to concede to 1.7 million yen.

After 10 days of tough negotiations between us, we reached an agreement that elderly persons aged 75 and older with an annual income of at least 2 million yen would be subject to an increase in out-of-pocket medical expenses from 10% to 20%. The increase will be implemented from October 2022. As a consequence, 3.7 million people will be affected, and this will reduce the burden on the working-age generation by about 100 billion yen annually.

Media outlets paid attention to the negotiations between the three of us and it was reported on TV news every day. Through these negotiations, I aimed at three points. First was to clarify KOMEITO's position. Second was to have people understand the process of the decision. Finally, the third was to show the presence of the KOMEITO.

Before December 21, 2020, the third 2020 supplementary budget bill with 30 trillion yen and the 2021 budget bill with 106 trillion yen were decided by the SUGA Cabinet. Since I had claimed a

ら、いくつかの問題があった。そのひとつは、原則1割となっている75歳以上の後期高齢者の医療費の窓口負担である。菅首相は、新たに2割負担を設定することを企図しており、それは現役世代の保険料を減らす狙いがある。

しかしながら、私は新型コロナウイルスの拡大を理由に、負担増加は延期すべきであり、また（仮に引き上げるとしても）2割負担は、単身で年間収入が240万円以上などの十分な収入がある方に限定すべきと主張した。

それでもなお、菅首相は、自民党の下村博文政務調査会長と田村憲久厚生労働大臣に、私（竹内）を説得して、（後期高齢者の年間収入が）170万円のラインまで譲歩するように強く命じたのである。

10日間にわたる三者の激しい交渉の末に、75歳以上の後期高齢者で少なくとも年間200万円以上の収入がある方を、医療費の窓口負担を2割に引き上げる対象とすることで合意をみた。引き上げは2022年の10月から実施されることになる。その結果、370万人の後期高齢者が影響を受け、これによって現役世代の負担を年間1,000億円減らすことになる。

メディアは我々三者の交渉に注目しており、連日テレビで報道されていた。この交渉を通して、私は3つのことを狙いとした。すなわち、第1に、公明党の立場を明確にすること。第2に、意思決定のプロセスを国民に理解してもらうこと。第3に、公明党の存在感を示すことであった。

2020年の12月21日までに、30兆円規模の2020年度第3次補正予算と、106兆円規模の2021年度予算案が、菅内閣によって閣議決定された。私はかねてより（経済の）需給ギャップを念頭に、両予算の規模を大きくするよう主張していたので、この結果は公明党を満足させるものとなった。両予算の主要政策は、新型コロナウイルス感染

large volume of both budgets with the supply-demand balance in mind, the result satisfied the KOMEITO. Major policies in both budgets consist of several pillars, such as countermeasures against novel coronavirus infections, digitalization, decarbonization, disaster prevention and so on. Many policies the KOMEITO had required were mostly realized.

The KOMEITO National Convention, Tokyo, September 27, 2020. TAKEUCHI was appointed Policy Chief.

Debate program on TV. (Tokyo, NHK)

症対策、デジタル化推進、脱炭素化、防災減災などいくつかの柱から構成されている。公明党が要求していた多くの政策はほとんど実現したのである。

菅首相へ提言（首相官邸）
Proposal to Prime Minister SUGA, Prime Minister's Office.

記者会見（首相官邸）
Press Conference, Prime Minister's Office.

The Growing Crisis of the SUGA Administration
（February 2021）

On January 7, 2021, Prime Minister SUGA declared a second state of emergency for 11 prefectures including Tokyo, due to a sharp increase of novel coronavirus infections. Last December, the government requested people to refrain from going outside unless it is absolutely necessary or urgent. However, from the end of 2020 to the beginning of 2021, large crowds were seen nationwide, especially in urban areas such as the Tokyo Metropolitan, Osaka City and Nagoya City.

The opposition parties started condemning the SUGA administration by saying that it was too late to declare another state of emergency. Surely, the number of coronavirus infections in Tokyo per day in early January continued to exceed 2,000, and as a result, beds for COVID-19 patients became scarce.

With the second state of emergency, the government requested restaurants and bars to close by 8 p.m., promising to pay ¥60,000 per day to every shop that cooperates. Moreover, the government is set to provide ¥400,000 to companies that deal with restaurants and bars, in cases where their sales decreased by half compared to the previous year.

Under such a tense atmosphere, we got breaking news. It was reported that two Diet members from the LDP and KOMEITO, visited hostess bars in the Ginza district of Tokyo late into the night, despite the state of emergency order. They both admitted visiting such bars.

Furthermore, it was revealed that this politician of the KOMEITO used his political fund for settling payment at a hostess bar. Not only concerning these two, but the LDP and the KOMEITO parties as a whole, came under fire.

As a consequence, he was forced to resign his seat. Besides, later, he was accused of illegal brokerage regarding a loan from the Japan Finance Corporation and his guilty verdict was upheld. Ethics are the bedrock for political parties, especially for the KOMEITO. Prime Minister SUGA himself was criticized for participating in two dinner gatherings last December while the government requested people to refrain from eating in large groups. The approval rate for the SUGA Cabinet has declined to 38% and the disapproval rate has risen to 43%.

How should we overcome these difficulties? First, we need to secure medical care for COVID-19 patients. Secondly, whether the human race can control the novel coronavirus depends on vaccinations. The Japanese government is set to approve the vaccine from U.S. pharmaceutical company Pfizer in mid-February and start inoculations for 3.7 million medical staff, then for approximately 36 million elderly people. In order for inoculations to succeed, it is important that the government and municipalities closely collaborate with each other.

Under the state of emergency, many people are suffering from the severe economic conditions. The KOMEITO proposed various measures to support these people to the government.

Nevertheless, the SUGA administration and the ruling parties face a crucial crisis in the weeks and months ahead.

Budget Committee, the House of Representatives, January, 2021.

COVID-19 Strategies of the KOMEITO

（February 2021）

Under the second state of emergency, the number of novel coronavirus infections per day has been declining since early February, 2021. Specifically, in Tokyo, which has kept infections below 500 for 7 consecutive days.

However, beds for COVID-19 patients have remained scarce as many patients are in serious conditions. As the Chairperson of the Policy Research Council of the KOMEITO, I have advised the government to continue the state of emergency until the number of novel coronavirus infections declines sufficiently per day. For example, in Tokyo, the number should be lower than 250. If the state of emergency is lifted too early, the novel coronavirus epidemic will again expand, leading to a fourth wave.

The approval rating for the SUGA Cabinet and the number of novel coronavirus infections seems to move in inverse proportion. Therefore, the government should prioritize containing the epidemic rather than restoring the economy for the time being.

At first, the government had prioritized the development of a Japanese vaccine, which delayed negotiations in securing vaccines from foreign pharmaceutical companies. Then, through the deliberation of the Budget Committee of the House of Councillors in March 2020, Mr. AKINO Kozo, a member of the KOMEITO party, proposed to procure vaccines from foreign pharmaceutical companies by using the 2020 fiscal year reserved budget. Following this proposal, the Vice Minister of Health, Labour and Welfare, Mr. INATSU Hisashi, who belongs to the KOMEITO, decided to negotiate with them.

As a consequence, the government succeeded in securing 314

公明党の新型コロナウイルス戦略

（2021 年 2 月）

　二度目の緊急事態宣言のもとで、1 日当たりの新型コロナウイルス感染者数は、2 月初旬以降減ってきている。特に東京では、7 日連続で 500 人を下回っている。

　しかしながら、新型コロナウイルス感染者用の病床は、重症患者数が高止まりしているために、依然として逼迫している。私は公明党の政務調査会長として、政府に対して、「1 日当たりの感染者数が十分に減少するまでは、緊急事態宣言を続けるべきである」とアドバイスしてきた。たとえば、東京では、感染者数が 1 日 250 人を下回るまでは続けるべきである。もしも、緊急事態宣言が早く解除されるならば、感染は再び拡大し、第 4 の波になるであろう。

　菅内閣の支持率と、新型コロナウイルス感染者数とは反比例しているように見える。したがって政府は、当面は経済の再建よりもむしろ、流行の抑制を優先すべきである。

　当初、政府は日本のワクチン開発を優先していたが、それによって、外国の製薬会社のワクチンを確保する交渉が遅れた。そこで、2020 年 3 月の参議院予算委員会の審議の中で、公明党の参議院議員の秋野公造氏が、予備費を活用して外国の製薬メーカーからワクチンを調達することを提案した。これを受けて、当時、厚生労働副大臣であった稲津久氏（公明党）が、外国の製薬会社と交渉することを決断したのだ。

　その結果、政府は 3 億 1,400 万回（1 億 5,700 万人）分のワクチンの確保に成功した（米国のファイザー社から 1 億 4,400 万回、英国のアストラゼネカ社から 1 億 2,000 万回、米国のモデルナ社から

million doses (157 million people) of coronavirus vaccines from U.S. Pfizer (144 million doses), U.K. AstraZeneca (120 million doses) and U.S. Moderna (50 million doses). The KOMEITO urged U.K. AstraZeneca to produce their vaccines in Japan through individual negotiations, which led to an announcement that AstraZeneca will consign a Japanese maker to produce vaccines.

Moreover, the KOMEITO persuaded the government to participate in the "COVAX FACILITY" which is a global framework led by the World Health Organization, aiming to provide vaccines to developing countries through a fund established by developed countries and private organizations. As a result, Foreign Minister MOTEGI Toshimitsu made the decision to provide $200 million to the "COVAX FACILITY".

Due to the lengthy affliction due to the novel coronavirus epidemic, many people have lost their jobs, and sales for small and medium-sized businesses have plummeted. The government has worked on various measures to stabilize employment, however, there are a lot of part-time employees who haven't received their wages.

The KOMEITO proposed additional measures for those in need to the government, such as individual loans of up to 2 million yen, benefits for renters, employment by local governments, stipends of up to 200,000 yen for university students, relaxation to conditions for receiving welfare payments, and so forth.

Subsequently, these policies were promptly implemented by the government. Furthermore, social isolation and loneliness are currently serious problems, which include various matters, such as domestic violence, single parents, care for the elderly and disabled, social withdrawal of youths, and so on. Therefore, the KOMEITO has proactively set up a team for preventing social isolation and loneliness. We will do our utmost efforts to solve these problems.

5,000万回）。公明党は、アストラゼネカ社と個別の交渉を通じて、同社に日本でのワクチン製造を促してきたが、これによって、同社は「日本のメーカーにワクチン生産の委託を行う」という発表に至った。

さらに公明党は、日本政府を説得して、世界保健機関（WHO）によって導入された世界的なフレームワークの「COVAX FACILITY（コバックス・ファシリティ）」に参加させたが、これは、先進国や民間団体によって設立されたファンドを通じて、発展途上国にワクチンを供給することが目的である。その結果、茂木敏充外務大臣は「コバックス・ファシリティ」に対して、日本政府から2億ドル（約200億円）を提供することを決定した。

新型コロナウイルス感染の長引く悪影響によって、多くの人々が職を失い、中小企業の売り上げは急落している。政府は雇用を安定化させるために様々な対策を講じているが、しかし、パート・アルバイトなど賃金を受け取っていない短期雇用者も多い。

そこで公明党として、政府に対して、困窮している人々への追加的施策を提案した。例えば、最大200万円までの個人貸付、住居確保給付金の支給、地方自治体による雇用、大学生への最大20万円までの給付、生活保護の需給要件の緩和、等々である。

その後、これらの政策は政府によって直ちに実現されることとなった。さらに、近年、社会的孤立や孤独が深刻な問題となっている。そこにはドメスティック・バイオレンスや、ひとり親、高齢者や障がい者への介護、若者の引きこもりなど、様々な課題が内包されている。公明党は社会的孤立や孤独を防ぐために、積極的に対策本部を立ち上げた。これらの問題を解決するために、最大限の努力をするつもりである。

Reaffirmation of the unbreakable Japan-U.S. Security Alliance
—U.S. President, from Trump to Biden
(March 2021)

Mr. Joe Biden was inaugurated as the 46th President of the United States of America on January 20, 2021. However, former president Donald Trump obtained around 74 million votes which chiefly reflected the voices of white Americans who were suffering from severe economic conditions. Mr. Trump, with no experience in public missions before assuming the presidency, was fond of making political deals like a business, and his administration management often astonishing people by his use of Twitter. His "America First" policies enhanced the presence of the U.S. while impeding China's ambitions on both economy and military fronts. He also withdrew the U.S. government from the "Trans Pacific Partnership (TPP)" and the "Paris Agreement" on climate change. It's no exaggeration to say that the Trump administration had further deepened divisions between the American people, for example the "Black Lives Matter" movement. Therefore, U.S. President Joe Biden has to now prioritize unification of the American people.

The Japan-U.S. Security Alliance is the cornerstone for peace, prosperity and freedom, not only for Japan but also for the Indo-Pacific region. Without this alliance, geopolitical circumstances would further increase instability in the South China Sea, the Korean Peninsula, and the Senkaku Islands of Japan. There are serious territorial disputes surrounding small islands in the South China Sea between Vietnam, Philippines and China. China has occupied these islands and built military bases. North Korea undoubtedly possesses nuclear weapons and ballistic missiles of all ranges, which further poses serious threats to South Korea and Japan.

強固な日米同盟の再確認
──米大統領はトランプからバイデンへ
（2021年3月）

　2021年1月20日、ジョー・バイデン氏が第46代米国大統領に就任した。しかし、前大統領のドナルド・トランプ氏も、厳しい経済状況に苦しんでいる白人の声を主に反映して約7,400万票を獲得したのである。大統領に就任するまで一度も公職の経験の無かったトランプ氏は、ビジネスと同様な政治的取引を好むとともに、彼の政権運営はしばしばツイッターの使用によって人々を驚かせてきた。彼の「アメリカファースト」政策は、経済と軍事における中国の野望を妨害しつつ、米国のプレゼンスを高めた。彼はまた、「環太平洋パートナシップ（TPP）」や、気候変動に関する「パリ合意」から米国政府を脱退させたのである。トランプ政権は、例えば、「ブラック・ライブズ・マター」運動のように、米国国民の分断をさらに深めたといっても過言ではない。したがって、バイデン大統領は、今は国民の団結を優先しなければならないのである。

　日米同盟は、日本のみならず、インド太平洋地域にとって、平和と繁栄と自由の礎である。もしもこの同盟が無ければ、南シナ海や朝鮮半島、また日本の尖閣諸島における地政学的状況は、さらに不安定さを増すであろう。南シナ海の小さな島々をめぐって、ベトナム・フィリピンと中国の間には深刻な領土問題が存在するが、中国はこれらの諸島を支配して軍事拠点を建設しているのだ。北朝鮮は、間違いなく核兵器とあらゆる射程の弾道ミサイルを保有しており、これらは韓国と日本に対してさらに深刻な脅威となっている。

　2021年1月、核兵器禁止条約が50カ国の批准を経て成立した。しかしながら、米国の核の傘のもとにある日本はこの条約を批准して

111

In January, 2021, the Nuclear Ban Treaty had gone into effect after ratification by 50 nations. However, Japan, which falls under the U.S. nuclear umbrella, has not joined the treaty. Given the deteriorating security environment in the East Asia region, it's difficult for Japan to ratify this treaty. However, I suppose that the role of Japan as the only nation to suffer atomic bombings should be to coordinate major nuclear powers and non-nuclear countries, which could lead to the abolition of nuclear weapons in the future. The KOMEITO urges the Japanese government to participate in the Nuclear Weapons Ban Treaty as an observer member.

Chinese Coast Guard vessels have repeatedly violated territorial waters surrounding the Senkaku Islands of Japan in the East China Sea, claiming territorial rights over these islands. However, the Biden administration announced the importance of the Japan-U.S. Alliance, and that Article 5 of the Japan-U.S. Security Treaty, which stipulates the obligation to defend Japan, would apply to the defense of the Senkaku Islands in Okinawa Prefecture. Furthermore, the U.S. underscored the importance of peace and stability in the Taiwan Strait and expressed serious concerns regarding the human rights situation in Hong Kong and the Xinjiang Uyghur Autonomous Region.

On March 12, 2021, Prime Minister SUGA took part in an online conference between the prime ministers of Australia, India, and president of the U.S. They confirmed that they share fundamental values to strengthen the international order based on the rule of law, supporting principles such as the peaceful resolution of disputes, democratic values and territorial integrity. Prime Minister SUGA is set to visit the U.S. and hold a Japan-U.S. summit meeting in April, which will be the first one for President Biden.

いない。東アジア地域の悪化する安全保障環境を考慮すると、日本がこの条約を批准することは困難である。しかしながら、私は唯一の被爆国としての日本の役割は、主要な核保有国と非保有国との間を調整することであり、このことが将来における核兵器の廃止につながるものと考えている。公明党は、日本政府に対して、核兵器禁止条約にオブザーバーとして参加するように促している。

中国海警局の船が、東シナ海の日本の尖閣諸島の領海にたびたび侵入し、これらの諸島の領有権を主張している。しかしながら、バイデン政権は日米同盟の重要性とともに、日本の防衛義務を規定している日米安全保障条約の第5条が、沖縄県の尖閣諸島の防衛にも適用されることを表明した。さらに、米国は、台湾海峡の平和と安定の重要性を強調したほか、香港と新疆ウイグル自治区における人権状況に関して、深刻な懸念を表明したのである。

2021年3月12日、菅首相はオーストラリアとインドの首相、そして米国大統領とのオンライン会議に参加。メンバーは、法の支配に基づく国際秩序を強化するために基本的な価値を共有すること、また紛争の平和的解決、民主主義の価値や、領土の一体性などの原則を支持することを確認した。菅首相は、4月に訪米し、日米首脳会談を開催する予定であるが、これはバイデン大統領にとって最初の首脳会談となるだろう。

日米首脳会談後、共同記者会見するバイデン米大統領（右）と菅首相（2021年4月16日、ワシントンのホワイトハウス、写真＝共同通信社）
U.S. President Biden and Prime Minister SUGA, joint press conference. (Photo: KyodoNews, White House Washington D.C., April 16, 2021)

Expedition of Domestic Vaccines against COVID-19
（April 2021）

The second state of emergency which was declared in Tokyo and 9 other prefectures on January 7, was lifted on March 21. It looked like the third wave of novel coronavirus epidemic had subsided for the moment. However, in Osaka prefecture, the number of coronavirus infections sharply increased at the beginning of April due to the spread of a mutated strain of the virus.

Currently, the biggest issue the Japanese people are concerned about is how to control the novel coronavirus infection. Therefore, the government and the ruling coalition need to present clear measures such as vaccinations, developments of medicine and PCR tests. From April 12, inoculations for the elderly (around 36 million people) is set to start. Vaccines for all Japanese people will be supplied by the U.S.'s Pfizer and Moderna, and the U.K.'s AstraZeneca.

Japanese pharmaceutical companies haven't yet succeeded in developing a vaccine against COVID-19, and are still at phase Ⅱ clinical trials. The reason for the delay is attributed to the many lawsuits against the side effects of vaccines, and a trial related to HIV-infected blood products. This is why the Ministry of Health, Labour and Welfare is prudent when approving new vaccines for COVID-19, and require pharmaceutical companies to implement large scale clinical trials in foreign countries. It's a serious issue that domestic vaccines against COVID-19 depend on foreign countries. The KOMEITO encourages the government to support Japanese pharmaceutical companies in the development of vaccines as early as possible.

Compared to the EU and the U.S., the number of coronavirus

114

国産コロナワクチン開発を急げ

（2021 年 4 月）

　1 月 7 日に、東京都や他の 9 府県で発出された 2 度目の緊急事態宣言は、3 月 21 日に解除された。それによって、新型コロナウイルスの 3 度目の波が、一瞬収束したかのように見えた。しかしながら、大阪府では、変異株の拡大が原因で、感染者数が 4 月初めから急増したのである。

　現在のところ、日本人が心配する最大の問題は、如何にして新型コロナウイルスの感染をコントロールするかである。したがって、政府与党は、ワクチン接種や薬の開発、PCR 検査など明確な手段を提示する必要がある。4 月 12 日から高齢者（3,600 万人）向けのワクチン接種が始まる予定である。すべての日本人のためのワクチンは、米国のファイザー社、モデルナ社、そして英国のアストラゼネカ社から供給されることになっている。

　日本の製薬会社は、まだコロナワクチンの開発に成功しておらず、まだ第 2 相の臨床試験の段階である。開発が遅れている理由は、これまでのワクチンの副反応に対する多くの訴訟や、HIV 感染血液製剤に関する裁判に起因している。このような理由から、厚生労働省は新しいコロナワクチンの承認に慎重であり、製薬会社に対して海外での大規模な臨床試験の実施を求めているのである。国内のコロナワクチンが外国に依存しているということは深刻な問題である。公明党は政府に対し、日本の製薬会社による早期のワクチン開発を支援するよう促している。

　EU や米国と比較して、日本の新型コロナウイルスの患者数や死者数は、極めて少ない。1 月 8 日時点で、英国における 1 日当たり

infections and fatalities of Japan are quite low. As of January 8, the number of coronavirus infections per day in the U.K. was around 70,000, while Japan was around 8,000. Subsequently, the U.K. rapidly improved their vaccination rollout in the following months, and around 39 million doses were administrated as of April 12. As a consequence, the number of coronavirus infections per day declined to around 3,000, which is around the same level of Japan. Vaccinations have proven to be effective against COVID-19.

However, it's very difficult for Japanese pharmaceutical companies to implement large scale clinical trials (from 30,000 to 40,000 subjects) in foreign countries. Given the vaccinations have already started overseas, ethical issues may occur. Even if it were possible, it will take several years for Japan to approve a domestic vaccine for COVID-19. That's way too late. If an sufficient increase in antibodies is seen in subjects in phase Ⅱ clinical trials for Japanese pharmaceutical makers compared to those from the U.S., the Ministry of Health, Labour and Welfare should consider approving a new vaccine.

の患者数は約 7 万人であったが、一方で日本は約 8,000 人であった。その後、英国の接種は数カ月で急速に進み、4 月 12 日の時点では約 3,900 万回の接種が行われた。その結果、1 日当たりの感染者数は約 3,000 人まで減少したが、それはだいたい日本と同水準である。ワクチン接種はコロナに有効であることが証明された。

　しかしながら、日本の製薬会社が、海外で 3 万〜 4 万人の大規模な臨床試験を実施することは困難となっている。海外ですでにワクチン接種が始まっていることを考慮すると、（海外での大規模臨床試験の実施は）倫理的な問題が起こるかもしれない。たとえそれが可能だとしても、日本が国産のコロナワクチンを承認するまでには数年かかることになるだろう。そのやり方では遅すぎるのである。もしも、日本の製薬メーカーによる第 2 相の臨床試験において、抗体が、米国ファイザー社と比べて十分に増加しているならば、厚生労働省は新しいワクチンの承認を検討すべきであろう。

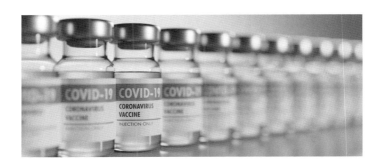

Major Policies for the 2021 General Election
（June 2021）

The present term for the members of the House of Representatives will expire on October 22, 2021. People are paying attention to when Prime Minister SUGA will dissolve the Lower House. Under the serious condition brought on by the novel coronavirus epidemic, the ruling coalition, the LDP and KOMEITO, have already started preparing for the general election. As the Chairperson for the Policy Research Council of the KOMEITO, I have formulated some basic thoughts regarding major policies for the 2021 general election.

First, we have to gain control over the novel coronavirus epidemic as early as possible. The government needs to secure ample vaccines for all people living in Japan and have them inoculated quickly. As of June 29, the number of people who have received their first shot of the coronavirus vaccine totaled over 28 million, while around 14 million people have received a second dose. The number of vaccinations per day has approached 1 million, which will raise the GDP around 1%. Moreover, the government must rebuild a firm medical system by securing healthcare staff, hospital beds and devices for future emergencies such as the coronavirus pandemic or other infectious diseases. Furthermore, it's important to develop domestic vaccines. For medical security, it is inadvisable that Japan depends on foreign vaccines. The KOMEITO will urge the government to help in the development of domestic coronavirus vaccines by Japanese pharmaceutical makers.

Second, the novel coronavirus pandemic revealed disparities and weaknesses in Japanese society including female non-regular workers and poverty. The KOMEITO will seek a society

2021 年衆議院議員総選挙の主要政策

(2021 年 6 月)

　現在の衆議院議員の任期は、2021 年 10 月 22 日までとなっており、菅首相がいつ衆議院を解散するかに注目が集まっている。新型コロナウイルスの流行によってもたらされた深刻な状況のもとで、連立与党の自民党と公明党はすでに総選挙の準備を始めている。私は、公明党の政務調査会長として、今回の総選挙の主要政策について基本的考え方をまとめてみた。

　第 1 に、新型コロナウイルスの流行を、できるかぎり早く収束させなければならないことだ。政府は日本に住むすべての人々のために十分なワクチンを確保し、迅速に接種する必要がある。6 月 29 日の時点では、1 回目のワクチン接種を受けた人の数は 2,800 万人を超えており、約 1,400 万人の人々が 2 回目の接種を受けている。1 日当たりの接種回数は 100 万回に近づいており、これによって GDP は約 1% 押し上げられるのである。その上で、政府は新型コロナウイルスの世界的大流行や、他の感染症など将来の緊急事態の場合に備えて、医療従事者、病床や医療機器を確保することで、しっかりとした医療体制を再構築しなければならない。さらに、国産ワクチンの開発は重要だ。医療安全保障のためには、日本が外国製のワクチンに依存することは望ましくない。公明党は、政府を促し、日本の製薬メーカーによる国産ワクチンの開発を支援する方針である。

　第 2 に、新型コロナウイルスの世界的大流行は、女性の非正規労働者や貧困など、日本社会が抱えていた格差や弱点を明らかにした。公明党は、SDGs の理念である「誰ひとり置き去りにしない」をもとに、女性がその能力やリーダーシップを発揮できる社会を追求してい

where females can increase their ability and leadership based on the SDGs principle "No one will be left behind". On May 31, we proposed a new plan to Prime Minister SUGA that 100,000 females can receive a digital education over three years, leading to future employment. The KOMEITO also insists on the use of different surnames for married couples if they choose, while the yeas and nays have been equally divided in the LDP.

Third, the KOMEITO intends to construct a new society through decarbonization and digitalization, which will overcome various issues the novel coronavirus revealed, bringing a driving force of a new growth. The KOMEITO insisted on a "Carbon Neutral Society in 2050" in the plenary session of the House of Representatives in January, 2020. Prime Minister SUGA ,who took office in September, agreed with this proposal and announced it as an international pledge. In order to implement this pledge, he decided to reduce greenhouse gases by 46% by 2030, compared to levels from 2013. However, this is not easy target to achieve. Therefore, I proposed to Prime Minister SUGA in the budget committee of the 2020 extraordinary Diet session in fall that the government should set up a large scale fund totaling ¥15 trillion for developing innovative technologies such as storage batteries, the use of hydrogen, carbon dioxide capture, utilization and storage. Soon after, SUGA accepted these proposals and established the "Green Innovation Fund" totaling 2 trillion yen. This fund will develop a new energy instead of relying on fossil fuels, and contribute to decarbonization, energy security and the creation of new industries and jobs.

The purpose of digitalization is to realize the successful livelihood of people and build a society where no one will be left behind. Digitalization (DX) is also a basic infrastructure for the government and private sector. Specifically, it is crucial for the "Social Security and Tax Number System (My Number card)",

く方針である。5 月 31 日には、「10 万人の女性が、将来の就労につ
ながるデジタル教育を 3 年間に亘り受けられるプラン」を、菅総理
に提出した。公明党はまた、当事者が希望するのであれば、「選択的
夫婦別姓」の使用を主張しているが、自民党ではこの問題に関して賛
否が真っ二つに分かれている。

　第 3 に、公明党は、脱炭素化やデジタル化を通して新しい社会を
構築していく方針であるが、これにより新型コロナウイルスが明らか
にした様々な問題が克服され、新しい成長に向かって勢いづくことに
なるだろう。公明党は、2020 年 1 月の衆議院代表質問で「2050 年二
酸化炭素排出実質ゼロ」を訴えた。9 月に就任した菅首相はこの提案
に同意し、国際公約として表明するとともに、この公約を実現するた
めに、「2013 年のレベルと比べて、2030 年には温室効果ガスを 46%
削減すること」を決定した。しかし、これは容易に達成される目標で
はない。そこで、私は 2020 年秋の臨時国会の予算委員会で、菅首相
に対して、「政府は蓄電池や水素の使用、二酸化炭素の回収・利用・
貯蔵（CCUS）などの革新的技術を発展させるため、15 兆円に及ぶ
大規模ファンドを立ち上げるべきだ」と提案した。菅首相は直ちにこ
の提案を受け入れて、2 兆円規模の「グリーン・イノベーション基金」
を創設したのである。この基金は、化石燃料に代わる新しいエネルギ
ーを開発するとともに、脱炭素化、エネルギー安全保障、そして新産
業と雇用を生み出すことに貢献するだろう。

　デジタル化の目的は、人々の豊かな暮らしと、誰ひとり置き去り
にしない社会を実現することである。デジタル化（DX）は、政府と
個人にとって基本的なインフラ（社会基盤）である。とりわけ、「社
会保障と税の番号制度（マイナンバーカード）」が重要であるが、そ
の加入率は、2020 年 12 月末の時点では 24% 程度に留まっている。
我々はさらに、カードを取得した人には最大で 100,000 円相当のポ

which enrollment has stalled at around 24 % as of June 30, 2021. We aim to further promote the use of the "My Number card" by granting up to 100,000 points to those who get the card. The "My Number card" has a firm system in place to prevent cyberattacks and leaks of the public information. The promotion of the card will generate large sources of revenue by urging administrative reform and streamlining social security.

Fourth, regarding parenting and education, the KOMEITO has emphasized a society which puts children's happiness first. We propose to establish a new administrative institution for children and their families, and enact a basic law for children. At the same time, the KOMEITO urges the government to set a commission that reflects children's voices through investigation, surveillance and advice concerning children's matters. Furthermore, we find it necessary to reduce parenting and educational expenses from childbirth to university.

Fifth, accelerated global warming has led to abnormal climate changes such as unprecedented typhoons, extreme deluges, and landslide disasters all over the world. Moreover, an earthquake in the capital and a Nankai trough earthquake are anticipated to occur in the near future. The KOMEITO promotes to bolster disaster prevention measures with a 15 trillion yen budget over the next 5 years.

The KOMEITO Manifesto for the 2021 General Election.
衆議院選挙の公明党の公約

イントを付与することによって、マイナンバーカードの普及を促進していくつもりである。マイナンバーカードは、サイバー攻撃と個人情報の流出を防ぐための強固なシステムを有している。マイナンバーカードの普及は、行政改革と社会保障の効率化を促し、大きな財源を生み出すことになるだろう。

第4に、公明党は子育てと教育に関して、子どもの幸福を最優先にする社会を重視してきた。我々は、「子どもと家庭のための新しい行政組織」を創設し、また「子ども基本法」を制定することを提案している。同時に、公明党は政府に対して、子どもの問題について調査、監視、勧告を通じて子どもの声を反映する「子どもコミッショナー」（第三者機関）を設立するよう促している。さらに、我々は出産から大学まで子育て・教育費用を軽減することが必要であると考えている。

第5に、加速化する地球温暖化が、世界中の前代未聞の台風や、大水害、土砂災害などの異常気象をもたらしている。加えて、首都直下型地震や南海トラフ地震が近い将来予測されている。（これらの状況を踏まえて）公明党は、向こう5年間で15兆円規模の予算を確保して防災対策を強化していく方針である。

衆議院選挙の公明党の公約発表（公明党代表、山口那津男〈左〉）
The release of the KOMEITO Manifesto for the 2021 General Election. YAMAGUCHI Natsuo, Representative of the KOMEITO (left).

Prime Minister SUGA and Factional Dynamics

（September 2021）

On September 3, 2021, Prime Minister SUGA Yoshihide abruptly announced that he wouldn't be running in the Liberal Democratic Party presidential race, which means his term as prime minister has come to an unexpected end. Mr. SUGA said that he will not run because he wants to focus on coronavirus measures and he considers it impossible to both work on the coronavirus measures and campaign. However, it seems that the real reason may be a little different.

Since his installation last September, several surging waves of the novel coronavirus have hit Japan hard, and as a result, the SUGA Cabinet's approval rating has slumped to the 30 % range. Many people have become increasingly frustrated with his administration's measures. Specifically, amid the fifth wave of coronavirus infections, which resulted in the highest number of confirmed cases per day topping 25,000. However, I suppose that whoever becomes prime minister will find it difficult to control the coronavirus epidemic, especially due to the Delta variant. Furthermore, the former Chairperson of Policy Research Council of the LDP, KISHIDA Fumio expressed his intent to run for the presidency.

In order to turn this situation around, Prime Minister SUGA planned to reshuffle the LDP's executive posts including Secretary-General Nikai, and some Cabinet members. Moreover, Mr. SUGA schemed to dissolve the House of Representatives after the party's executive appointments in mid-September. This confidential information was revealed by a media outlet.

It is reported that KOIZUMI Shinjiro, Minister of Environment, opposed SUGA's advances to dissolve the House of Representatives, as an escape from the LDP's presidential race and a contradiction of SUGA's former promise to prioritize the coronavirus measures. Mr. SUGA had no choice to but to abandon the idea of a snap election. Nevertheless, he sought to reshuffle the LDP's executive posts, but he found it difficult and finally gave up.

Mr. SUGA doesn't belong to, nor dose he have his own faction among the LDP Diet members. Therefore, he had to depend on other factions such as the HOSODA (ABE), ASO and NIKAI groups. However, Mr. SUGA couldn't shore up support from any factions. They were not confident of SUGA's victory in the presidential race. It is no exaggeration to say that Mr. SUGA was at the mercy of factional dynamics. However, as a consequence to Mr. SUGA bowing out, the LDP's approval rating has been sharply rising due to expectations of his successor. On the other hand, approval ratings of the opposition parties have been declining.

As of September 17, the former Chairperson of Policy Research Council KISHIDA Fumio, Minister of Regulatory Reform KONO Taro, former Minister of Internal Affairs and Communications TAKAICHI Sanae, and Executive Acting Secretary-General NODA Seiko announced their intensions to run for the presidential race, which is set to start on September 17, with voting to take place on the 29.

Both the public and opposition parties have been paying special attention to the LDP presidential election. The opposition parties, especially the Constitutional Democratic Party of Japan has become increasingly impatient. We can't anticipate who will win. The new LDP President will be elected as the 100th prime minister in the Diet and the KOMEITO is set to conclude an agreement for the new LDP-KOMEITO administration. Soon after, the new prime minister will dissolve the Houses of Representatives mid-October.

KISHIDA Fumio was elected as the 100th Prime Minister of Japan
—Why couldn't the opposition parties win the 2021 General Election?
(November 2021)

Mr. KISHIDA Fumio, former Chairperson of the Policy Research Council of the Liberal Democratic Party (LDP), defeated Mr. KONO Taro, Minister of Regulatory Reform, in the final ballot of the LDP presidential race on September 29. He was then elected as the 100th prime minister of Japan in the Diet on October 4.

Mr. KISHIDA formed his cabinet on October 6, and soon he announced the dissolution of the House of Representatives on October 14 with voting to take place on October 31. This decision disrupted the oppositions strategy for the coming election as many anticipated the election to take place between November 7 and 14.

The fifth wave of coronavirus epidemic drastically weakened in early October, due to an increase in vaccinations and the administration of pharmaceutical therapies for COVID-19. Specifically, the number of vaccinations per day topped one million to 1.6 million in October. As of October 31, the percentage of vaccinated people who received their second dose reached close to 70%, and as a consequence, Japan advanced to fifth place in world ratings for vaccination. The use of cocktail antibody treatment, called "Casirivimab / Imdevimab" was very effective in curbing the multiplication of the coronavirus.

During the election campaign, opposition parties, such as the Constitutional Democratic Party (CDP) and the Japan Communist Party (JCP), bitterly claimed the LDP-KOMEITO administration failed in taking proper countermeasures against COVID-19. However, the opposition parties have no right to criticize the ruling parties. At first, the opposition parties rejected the early approval of coronavirus vaccines from Pfizer and Moderna, requiring large

126

岸田文雄氏が第 100 代首相に就任
——なぜ野党は衆議院議員総選挙で勝利できなかったのか
（2021 年 11 月）

　9 月 29 日に行われた自民党総裁選の決戦投票で、自由民主党の前政務調査会長の岸田文雄氏は、前規制改革担当大臣の河野太郎氏を破った。その後、彼は 10 月 4 日に国会で第 100 代首相に選ばれた。

　岸田氏は 10 月 6 日に内閣を組閣した後、直ちに、14 日に衆議院を解散し、31 日に投開票を行うと宣言した。多くの人々は衆院選が11 月 7 日から 14 日の間に行われると予想していたので、この決断は野党の衆院選の戦略を躓かせることになった。

　コロナウイルス流行の第 5 波は、ワクチン接種の増加とコロナウイルス治療薬の投与のおかげで、10 月初めには劇的に弱まった。特に、1 日当たりのワクチン接種数は、10 月には 100 万回を超え最大160 万回にまで昇ったのである。10 月 31 日の時点では、ワクチンを2 回接種した人々の割合が 70％に近づいており、その結果、日本の接種率は世界で 5 位に入っている。カシリビマブとイムデビマブの抗体カクテル療法が、コロナウイルスの増殖を抑えるのに大変有効であった。

　衆議院選挙の中で、立憲民主党や日本共産党などの野党は、自公政権がコロナ禍に対して、正しい対策を講ずることに失敗したと激しく責め立てた。しかしながら、野党に与党を非難する資格は無い。当初、野党はファイザー社やモデルナ社のコロナワクチンの早期承認を拒否し、日本での大規模治験を要求していた。野党はまた、1 日当たり100 万回のワクチン接種にも、自治体が実行することが困難であるという理由で反対していたのだ。

　1 日当たりのコロナウイルス感染者数は 9 月初めから減少し、11

clinical trials in Japan. They also opposed the vaccination roll out by the government of one million shots per day because it was too difficult for municipalities to implement.

The number of confirmed coronavirus cases per day has declined since early September, and as of November 15, there were only 79 cases reported across the nation. Meanwhile, the approval ratings for the LDP and KOMEITO have steadily improved since October.

Mr. EDANO Yukio, Chief Representatives of the CDP, announced his strategy of cooperating with the JCP to field unified candidates in single seat districts. However, there are definite differences regarding basic policies between the two parties. According to the platform of the JCP, the Japan- U.S. Security Treaty and the Self Defense Force (SDF) are unconstitutional, while the CDP considers them as constitutional. On October 19, when the election campaign started, North Korea launched two ballistic missiles towards the Sea of Japan. The ruling bloc criticized the CDP-JCP coalition on how to defend Japan without the Japan-U.S. Security Treaty and the SDF. YOSHINO Tomoko, leader of the Japanese Trade Union Confederation, also condemned the CDP-JCP coalition.

Prime Minister KISHIDA put forth a policy, "New Capitalism" that will realize a "virtuous cycle of growth and distribution". He stressed "We will improve productivity through a growth strategy and distribute the fruits to workers in the form of higher wages, broadly raising the income level of the people".

The KOMEITO agreed with his proposals, and proposed during the general election that the government should distribute ¥ 100,000 to all children aged 0-18. The KOMEITO aims to realize a child-first society that prioritizes their happiness. It's an ideal that every child should be raised equally, irrelevant of their parents' income. Many children and their parents have suffered from the coronavirus epidemic. Supporting children will lead to the development of the nation and stabilize social security. Moreover,

月 15 日には国内で報告された感染者数は、わずか 79 人に過ぎなく
なった。その一方で、自民党と公明党の支持率は 10 月から着実に上
昇していったのである。

　立憲民主党代表の枝野幸男氏は、日本共産党と小選挙区での候補者
を一本化するという戦略を発表した。しかしながら、両党の間には基
本政策に関して明確な違いがある。日本共産党の綱領によれば、「日
米安全保障条約と自衛隊は違憲である」とされているが、他方、立憲
民主党はこれらを「合憲」であるとしている。10 月 19 日選挙戦が公
示日となりスタートした時、北朝鮮は 2 発の弾道ミサイルを日本海
に向け発射した。与党は立憲民主党・日本共産党連合に対して、「日
米安全保障条約や自衛隊無くして、どうやって日本を守るのか」と批
判した。日本労働組合総連合の芳野友子会長もまた、立憲・共産連合
を非難した。

　岸田首相は、成長と分配の好循環を実現する「新しい資本主義」の
政策を前面に打ち出した。首相は、成長戦略を通じて生産性を高め、
その果実をより高い賃金の形で労働者に分配し、幅広く人々の所得水
準を引き上げることを強調する。

　公明党は首相の提案に賛成した上で、選挙戦では「18 歳以下の全
ての子どもに、政府が 10 万円を支給すべきである」と提案した。公
明党は、「子どもの幸福を最優先する社会」の実現を目指している。
それは、一人ひとりの子どもは、親の収入に関係なく平等に育てられ
るべきであるという理想だ。多くの子どもたちとその親は、コロナウ
イルスの流行で苦しんできた。社会全体で子どもたちを支えることは、
国の発展につながり社会保障を安定させる。さらに、公明党は総選挙
で「マイナンバーカードを取得した個人に対して、3 万円相当のポイ
ントを付与する」ことを公約に掲げた。これは、マイナンバーカード
を普及させるとともに消費を喚起することが狙いであり、それによっ

The KOMEITO pledged in the general election to grant shopping points worth 30,000 yen per person to those who get the "My Number cards". This aims to promote the "My Number cards" and stimulate consumption, which will prompt digitalization for society and administrative reform. These policies undoubtedly contributed to the victory for the KOMEITO party.

The opposition coalition pledged to reduce the consumption tax rate from 10% to 5% and exempt people from income tax for one year. However, it seems to me that most people didn't expect their promise to be realized.

On October 31, the LDP and the KOMEITO secured 293 seats (LDP 261; KOMEITO 32), which brought a stable majority to the ruling bloc in the 465-seat House of Representatives. The LDP decreased from 291 to 261, while the KOMEITO increased from 29 to 32. Before election day, media outlets forecasted that the LDP will decrease to about 220. Therefore, they considered that the KOMEITO pushed up the LDP members who were in severe contests for their single seat constituencies. It was a right understanding. The CDP declined from 109 to 96 and the JCP also lost two seats, from 12 to 10. On the other hand, the Japan Innovation Party (JIP) increased from 11 to 41. People criticizing the LDP might have voted for the JIP, since they disliked the cooperation between the CDP and the JCP. The JIP mainly insists on administrative reform or decentralization, but it is not necessarily definite what type of nation they intend to create.

UPDATE: Surprisingly, on November 6, 2022, former Chief Representative of the CDP, EDANO Yukio announced "It was a mistake that the CDP pledged to temporarily reduce the consumption tax rate from 10% to 5% in the 2021 general election".

て社会のデジタル化や行政改革を促進することになるだろう。これらの政策が、公明党の勝利に貢献したことは疑い無い。

　野党連合は、1 年限り消費税率を 10％から 5％へ引き下げることや、所得税をゼロにすることを公約した。しかしながら、ほとんどの国民は野党連合の公約は実現することは無いと観たようだ。

　10 月 31 日、自民党と公明党は計 293 議席（自民党 261、公明党 32）を獲得したが、これは衆議院 465 議席の中で、与党に対して安定多数をもたらすことになった。自民党は選挙前の 291 議席から 261 議席へと減らしたが、公明党は 29 議席から 32 議席へと増やした。投票日前にマスメディアは、自民党は 220 議席まで減るだろうと予測していた。したがって、マスメディアは、小選挙区で厳しい状況にある自民党の候補者を、公明党が押し上げたとみなしたのである。それは正しい認識だ。

　立憲民主党は選挙前の 109 議席から 96 議席へと減らし、日本共産党もまた 2 議席を失い、12 議席から 10 議席へと後退した。その一方で、日本維新の会は、11 議席から 41 議席へと躍進した。自民党を批判していた人々は、立憲民主党と日本共産党の協力を嫌って、日本維新の会に投票したのかもしれない。日本維新の会は、主に行政改革や地方分権を主張しているが、どのような国を作ろうとしているのかは、必ずしも明確ではないのである。

（後日談）

　驚くことに、2022 年 11 月 6 日、前立憲民主党の枝野幸男代表は、「2021 年の衆議院選挙で、消費税率を一時的に 10％から 5％へ引き下げると公約したことは誤りであった」と表明したのである。

What is "New Capitalism"?
(February 2022)

Since early January, 2022, the number of confirmed Omicron variant cases has sharply increased. On February 5, cases topped 100,000, the highest ever and nearly four times as much as the fifth wave last year. The Omicron variant is highly infectious, while the rate of severe cases remain low. However, if the virus spreads rapidly among the elderly and those with co-morbidities, the rate of severe cases may increase.

The approval rate of the KISHIDA cabinet depends on whether the government can control the spread of the Omicron variant. The government has already applied quasi-state of emergencies to prevent the further spread of COVID-19 to the 35 prefectures and will promote booster shots.

Prime Minister KISHIDA advocated "New Capitalism" in his policy speech in the ordinary Diet session. What is "New Capitalism"? According to his statements, an excessive market economy has brought with it disparities among people and climate change. Mr. KISHIDA stressed "New Capitalism will realize a virtuous cycle of growth and distribution. We will improve productivity through growth strategy, and distribute the fruits to workers in the form of wages, broadly raising income levels of people".

The KOMEITO agrees with his idea, especially by putting emphasis on distribution. The KOMEITO believes it is necessary to overcome deflation, making it possible to raise wages. As of September 2021, the gap between supply and demand was deemed approximately 27 trillion yen. Therefore, the government has to compensate this gap by implementing the fiscal year 2021

「新しい資本主義」とは何か

（2022 年 1 月）

　2022 年の 1 月初めから、確認されたコロナウイルスのオミクロン株の感染者数は急激に増加している。2 月 5 日には感染者数は 10 万人を超えて、これまでで最も高く、昨年の第 5 波の 4 倍にも達している。オミクロン変異株は感染力が高いものの、重症者は少ない。しかし、高齢者や基礎疾患のある人々にウイルスが急速に広がれば、重症者数の割合は増えていくだろう。

　岸田内閣の支持率は、政府がオミクロン変異株の感染をコントロールできるかどうかにかかっている。政府はすでに 35 の都道府県に、コロナのさらなる感染拡大を防ぐため、まん延防止等重点措置を適用するとともに、3 回目の接種を促進していく方針だ。

　岸田首相は、通常国会の施政方針演説で「新しい資本主義」を提唱した。「新しい資本主義」とは何だろうか。彼の演説によると、「行きすぎた市場経済は、人々の間に格差と気候変動をもたらした」「新しい資本主義は、成長と分配の好循環を実現する。成長戦略を通じて生産性を高めるとともに、賃金という形でその果実を労働者に分配し、幅広く人々の所得を向上させる」と強調する。

　公明党は岸田首相の考えに同意しているが、特に分配を重視している。公明党は、デフレーションを克服することが必要であり、それが賃金引き上げを可能にすると考える。2021 年 9 月の段階での需給ギャップは、およそ 27 兆円と推計されている。したがって、政府は、2021 年度補正予算と 2022 年度当初予算を執行することで、このギャップを埋め合わせる必要がある。

　日本は、約 20 年間デフレに苦しんできた。デフレの原因は、供給

supplementary budget and the 2022 initial budget.

Japan has suffered from deflation for around 20 years. The cause for deflation is said to be a shortage of demand compared to supply. Demand depends on money supply. Therefore, in order to overcome deflation, distribution is very important. Actually, for the past two years during the coronavirus pandemic, the government prepared and implemented economic measures totaling 80 trillion yen. As a consequence, the government was able to prevent many corporate bankruptcies and keep Japan's unemployment rate the lowest among OECD nations. Moreover, tax revenue during these two years increased by 8.5 trillion yen including corporate, income and consumption tax. It was an unprecedented phenomenon that tax revenue increased as the GDP decreased. This proves the accuracy of our proactive fiscal policy.

Regarding investment in human resources, the government has thus far supported non-regular employees in becoming regular employees and is set to secure 400 billion yen over three years and create a new system for part-time and temporary workers who want to change jobs, as well as those who lost their jobs as non-regular employees.

Prime Minister KISHIDA urged the Japan Business Federation (Keidanren) to raise wages by more than 3%. The KOMEITO is set to propose in the 2022 House of Councillors election that the government should set up a "Third Committee" which consists of economic scholars elected by labor and management to indicate the target for raising wages in the spring labor-management negotiations. Continuous raising wages will make it possible to overcome inflation and to reconstruct Japanese finances.

The KOMEITO claims that the most critical investment in human resources is raising children and education. In the near future, we are set to formulate the "Child-Rearing Support Master Plan" through the research and deliberation over the period of

に対して需要が不足していることである。需要はマネーサプライに依存している。したがって、デフレを克服するには分配が大変重要である。実際に、過去2年間コロナ禍の中で、政府は合計80兆円に及ぶ経済対策を準備し、実行してきた。その結果、政府は多くの倒産を防ぎ、日本の失業率をOECD各国の中でも最も低い水準に維持することができたのだ。それだけではない。税収はこの2年間で、法人税、所得税、消費税を含めて8.5兆円も増加したのである。GDPが減少したにもかかわらず税収が増加したというのは、前代未聞の現象である。これは我々の積極財政の正しさを証明していることになる。

人への投資に関しては、政府は、これまで非正規雇用労働者が正社員化することを支援してきたが、今後3年間で4,000億円を確保して、非正規雇用労働者が失業した時と同様に、転職を希望するパートや派遣労働者のための新しいシステムを創る予定だ。

岸田首相は日本経団連にも3%以上の賃金引き上げを促した。公明党は、2022年の参議院選挙では、労使双方から選ばれた経済学者からなる「第三者委員会」を創設し、春闘の労使交渉において賃金引上げの目安を提示すべきだと提案する予定である。継続的な賃上げは、インフレーションの克服と日本の財政再建を可能にするだろう。

最も重要な人への投資は「子育てと教育」であるというのが公明党の主張だ。我々は、2年に及ぶ調査と議論を経て、子育てと教育支援のための「子育て応援トータルプラン」をまもなく発表する予定である。このプランでは、子どもの幸福を最優先として、妊娠から大学卒業までの親の負担の軽減や無償化、男女の不平等の解消、若者への経済的支援や、より良いワークライフ・バランスなど、具体的な対策を提案するつもりである。

デジタル化は、成長と分配の好循環にとって鍵となる役割を果たすだろう。ところが、新型コロナウイルスの世界的大流行によって、日

two years. This plan aims to prioritize the happiness of children by proposing concrete measures such as reducing or eliminating the burdens on parents from pregnancy to college graduation, dissolution of inequality between males and females, economic aid for young people and a better work-life balance.

Digitalization will play a key role for a virtuous cycle of growth and distribution. However, the novel coronavirus pandemic uncovered the delay in digitalization in Japanese society. The backbone for digitalization is the "My Number card". The KOMEITO pledged in the 2021 general election to promote the "My Number card" for social digitalization by granting points worth up to 30,000 yen to those who get the card. Digitalization will improve productivity and accelerate raising wages.

A balance between the human race and nature is important, as stated in the KOMEITO party's platform. Mr. SAITO Tetsuo, secretary-general of the KOMEITO at that time, insisted on a "Carbon Neutral Society by 2050" in the plenary session of the House of Representatives in January 2020. The KOMEITO is the only political party to propose a "Carbon Neutral Society in 2050" in the Diet. Former Prime Minister SUGA , who took office in September, agreed with this proposal and announced it as an international pledge. In order to implement this pledge, he decided to reduce greenhouse gases by 46% by 2030, compared to levels from 2013. This is a historical achievement.

Thus, the KOMEITO aims to construct a social-economic system that people can really experience happiness by correcting various issues brought on by capitalism such as disparity and poverty, and serious climate change. This is the answer to "New Capitalism".

本社会のデジタル化の遅れが露呈した。デジタル化の基盤となるものは「マイナンバーカード」である。そこで公明党は、2021年の衆院選では、社会のデジタル化のために「マイナンバーカード」を普及することを公約に掲げ、その際カード取得者に最大3万円相当のポイントを付与することとした。デジタル化は企業の生産性を高めるとともに、賃上げを加速するだろう。

公明党の綱領には「人間と自然の調和」の重要性が明記されている。公明党の斉藤鉄夫幹事長（当時）は、「2050年までにカーボンニュートラル（脱炭素化）社会を実現すること」を2020年1月の衆議院代表質問で主張した。公明党は国会で「2050年脱炭素社会実現」を提案した唯一の政党である。9月に就任した菅前首相はこの提案に賛同し、国際公約として表明するとともに、この公約を具体化するために「2030年までに、2013年と比べて温室効果ガスを46％削減すること」を決定したのである。これは歴史的な業績である。

このように公明党は、格差や貧困、深刻な気候変動問題などの資本主義の課題を是正し、国民が幸福を実感できる社会経済システムの構築を目指している。これが「新しい資本主義」に対する回答である。

衆議院予算委員会での代表質問
（2021年12月13日）
Budget Committee, the House of
Representatives, December 13, 2021.

Russia's Invasion of Ukraine (1)
—This is Putin's War
（March 2022）

Russia abruptly launched an aggresive attack against Ukraine on February 24, 2022. To hear of this news at the Prime Minister's office, I was both heartbroken and dumbstruck. Russia's invasion of Ukraine is an outrageous violation of international law and tramples on the principles of sovereignty and territorial integrity. We can never accept such an attempt to change the status quo by force.

German Chancellor, Scholz strongly criticized Russian President Putin by saying, "He alone, not the Russian people, chose this war. He alone bears full responsibility for this. This war is Putin's war." in the emergency video conference of the G7 held on February 24.

A joint statement from the G7 announced severe and coordinated economic and financial sanctions against Russia. Furthermore, the EU, the U.S., Canada and Japan decided to exclude several Russian banks from the Society for Worldwide Interbank Telecommunications (SWIFT) network, where more than 10,000 financial institutions worldwide exchange information for money transfers. These sanctions will deal a blow to the Russian economy. However, NATO and the U.S. have no intension to directly intervene in this war, since they fear the risk of military escalation potentially leading to World War Ⅲ. So far, western nations have been stepping up their military assistance for the Ukrainian troops engaged in war with Russian forces.

Russian troops first attacked Ukrainian military facilities with missiles aiming to siege large cities like the capital Kyiv, and the second largest city, Kharkiv. However, they were met with strong resistance by Ukrainian troops, and as a consequence, their

ロシアのウクライナ侵略（1）
——これはプーチンの戦争だ
（2022 年 3 月）

2022 年 2 月 24 日、ロシアは突如ウクライナへの侵略を開始した。私は首相官邸でこのニュースを聞き、ショックを受けるとともに言葉を失った。ロシアによるウクライナへの侵略は、国際法に違反する暴挙であるとともに、主権と領土を蹂躙（じゅうりん）するものである。我々は力による現状変更の試みを、決して受け入れることはできない。

ドイツ首相のショルツ氏は、ロシアのプーチン大統領を批判して、「ロシアの人民ではなく、彼だけが、この戦争を選んだのだ。彼だけがこの戦争に責任がある。この戦争はプーチンの戦争だ」と、同月 24 日に開かれた G7 の緊急ビデオ会議で述べた。

G7 の共同声明では、各国の協調のもとに、ロシアに対する厳しい経済、金融制裁が発表された。さらに、EU、米国、カナダそして日本は、世界の 1 万以上の金融機関が、送金情報をやり取りする国際銀行間通信協会（SWIFT）のネットワークから、ロシアの複数の銀行を排除することを決定した。これらの制裁はロシア経済に打撃となるだろう。しかしながら、NATO や米国は、潜在的に第三次世界大戦につながる軍事的エスカレーションのリスクを恐れて、この戦争に直接介入する意図は無い。今のところ、西側諸国は、ロシア軍と戦闘状態にあるウクライナ軍への軍事的支援を強化しつつある。

ロシア軍は当初、ミサイルでウクライナの軍事施設を攻撃し、首都キーウや、第二の都市ハルキウのような大都市を包囲することを目論んでいた。しかしながら、ウクライナ軍の激しい抵抗にあい、その結果、ウクライナへの地上侵略は行き詰まっている。劇場や学校に避難

ground invasion of Ukraine has stalled. Many civilians who took shelter in theaters and schools were wounded or died by these bombings, which is a war crime against humanity.

As of March 20, the number of refugees from Ukraine is over 3 million. Moreover, Russian troops occupied nuclear power plants such as Chernobyl and Zaporizhazia.

Negotiations for a ceasefire between Russia and Ukraine have stalled. Russia demands Ukraine disarmament and preserves a position of neutrality, while Ukraine refuses calling for an immediate ceasefire and a withdrawal of Russian troops. Despite negotiations, fierce urban warfare has continued through Mariupol in southeast Ukraine, where Russian troops have sieged. It was reported that over 3,000 civilians died by indiscriminate assaults by Russian forces and at least 200,000 people, almost equivalent to half of the population, still remain in Mariupol.

Due to the extremely cold weather, many people including children, have taken refuge in underground shelters where there is hardly any food and water, medicine, heaters or communications.

Ukraine President, Volodymyr Oleksandrovych ZELENSKYY clearly stated that Ukraine will never surrender to Russia. He made several addresses online with Legislatures of foreign countries, such as the U.S., the U.K., Germany and Canada. On March 22, Japanese Diet members are set to hear his speech online.

Due to restraints of the Constitution of Japan, Japan is unable to provide any military support to Ukraine. Therefore, the government decided to provide 200 million dollars to Ukraine as humanitarian aid, and helping people flee from the war to Japan. Since the war is at a deadlock, concerns are growing on whether Russia will escalate further assaults or use biological and chemical weapons. In order to stop this war, Japan will make every effort for a peaceful resolution with the close cooperation of international communities.

していた多くの市民が爆撃で死傷したが、これは人道に対する戦争犯罪である。

3月20日の時点で、ウクライナからの避難者数は300万人を超えている。さらに、ロシア軍はチェルノブイリ（チョルノービリ）や、ザポリージャの原子力発電所を占拠したのである。

ロシアとウクライナの停戦交渉は難航している。ロシアはウクライナに対して、軍備解除と中立化を要求しているが、ウクライナは拒否し、即時停戦とロシア軍の撤退を主張している。交渉にもかかわらず、ロシア軍が包囲した南東ウクライナのマリウポリでは、激しい市街戦が続いている。ロシア軍の無差別攻撃によって、3,000名を超える市民が死亡し、人口のほぼ半分に匹敵する少なくとも20万人がマリウポリに留まっていると伝えられている。

極寒の天候のもと、子供を含む多くの人々が地下のシェルターに避難しているが、そこでは食べ物、水、薬、暖房、また通信手段のほとんどが欠乏している有様だ。

ウクライナのゼレンスキー大統領は、「ウクライナは絶対にロシアに屈することはない」と明確に述べている。大統領は米国、英国、ドイツ、カナダなど、いくつもの外国の国会でもオンラインで演説を行っており、3月22日には、日本の国会議員はオンラインで大統領のスピーチを聞くことになっている。

日本は憲法上の制約によって、ウクライナに対して軍事上の支援をすることはできない。したがって、政府はウクライナに人道支援として2億ドルを供与するとともに、日本への避難民への支援を決定している。戦争が暗礁に乗り上げているため、ロシアが攻撃を激化させるか、あるいは生物化学兵器を使用する懸念が増大している。この戦争を止めるために、日本は国際社会と緊密に連携し、平和的解決に全力を尽くすつもりである。

Russia's Invasion of Ukraine (2)
—Hard Resistance by Ukraine forces
（April 2022）

Japanese Diet members attended the online address given by Ukrainian President Zelenskyy on March 23, 2022, where I also participated as policy chief of the KOMEITO party. I keenly felt that Zelenskyy's facial expressions revealed his severe resolution to fight against the Russian military, even at the risk of his own life. He extended his gratitude for the aid and called on Japan to continue its economic sanctions against Russia. He pointed out the dysfunction of the United Nations Security Council on the brink of crisis and in need for reform. He also asked Japan to play a major role to reform the U.N.

Due to hard resistance by the Ukrainian troops, Russian forces aiming to siege the capital Kyiv had no choice but to withdraw in late March. However, mass killings of civilians in Bucha and other Ukrainian cities near Kyiv were revealed. On April 12, 403 bodies were found in Bucha. The number of fatalities in Mariupol in southeastern Ukraine topped 10,000 and may even exceed 20,000. There have been many civilian bodies left on the streets. Fierce urban warfare has continued night and day, and the situation is rather disadvantageous for Ukraine.

U.S. President Biden expressed his view that Russia's aggression against Ukraine is "Genocide". The Organization for Security and Cooperation in Europe (OSCE) released a report on April 13 that confirmed the definite violation against international and humanitarian laws by Russian forces. The report pointed out that regarding the assaults on the hospital and theater in Mariupol, the person in charge committed war crimes since there were no effective warnings or times for evacuation. The OSCE

ロシアのウクライナ侵略（2）
──ウクライナ軍の激しい抵抗
（2022 年 4 月）

　2022 年 3 月 23 日、日本の国会議員はウクライナのゼレンスキー大統領の演説をオンラインで聴くこととなったが、そこには、私も公明党の政務調査会長として参加した。私は、ゼレンスキー大統領の表情から、彼が命懸けでロシア軍と戦う決意であることを痛切に感じた。大統領は日本の支援に感謝するとともに、日本がロシアに対する制裁を継続するよう訴えた。彼はまた、国連安保理が危機にあって機能不全に陥っており、その改革の必要性を指摘するとともに、日本が国連改革の重要な役割を果たすよう要請したのである。

　ウクライナ軍の激しい抵抗にあい、首都キーウを取り囲んでいたロシア軍は 3 月下旬に撤退を余儀なくされた。しかし、キーウ近郊のブチャその他の諸都市では、市民の大量虐殺が明らかになったのである。4 月 12 日、ブチャでは 403 人の遺体が発見された。ウクライナ南東部のマリウポリでの死傷者数は、1 万人を超えており、最悪 2 万人を超えるかもしれない。多くの市民の遺体が路上に放置されたままである。激しい市街戦が昼夜を問わず続いており、ウクライナにとってかなり不利な情勢となっている。

　米国のバイデン大統領は、ロシアのウクライナへの侵攻は「ジェノサイド（大量虐殺）」だとの見解を表明した。欧州安全保障協力機構（OSCE）は、4 月 13 日、ロシア軍による、国際人道法に対する明らかな違反であることを確認したとの報告書を発表した。報告書では、マリウポリでの病院や劇場に対する攻撃について、責任者は避難のための効果的な警告や期限を設けておらず、戦争犯罪を遂行したと指摘している。OSCE は、拷問など人権に対するほとんどの違反は、

found reliable evidence that most violations against human rights like torture, were done in the region or under the organization occupied by Russian troops.

On the other hand, Russian President Putin said, "It was fake news". "It's impossible to isolate Russia" and "Russia couldn't avoid military aggression against Ukraine to save the people in the eastern Ukraine".

Since early April, Russian troops have been moving to the eastern and southeastern parts of Ukraine. They have initially aimed for the surrender of Kyiv. However, due to fierce resistance by Ukrainian forces and logistical problems, Russian troops seemed to change their strategy and are now focusing on suppressing the southeastern port city of Mariupol. They aim to take control of Donetsk and Luhansk in the east while Ukraine forces achieved a brilliant success in the sinking of the Russian missile cruiser, "Moscow".

As of April 22, Russian troops have almost taken control of Mariupol, sieging the ironworks factory where Ukrainian forces barricaded themselves with refugees. Putin aims to complete the occupation of Donetsk and Luhansk by May 9, the anniversary of the victory over Nazi Germany in World War II.

However, the Biden administration announced additional military aid of 800 million dollars to Ukraine and the EU decided to provide 500 million euros.

Prime Minister KISHIDA Fumio announced additional sanctions over Russia's invasion of Ukraine, such as the freezing of assets of Russia's largest bank, Sberbank, a ban on Russian coal imports and the deportation of diplomats from the Russian Embassy in Japan. KISHIDA stated "We are at a critical point to bring an end to the inhuman aggression and protect our order of peace".

ロシア軍によって占領された地域や組織のもとでなされたことを示す、信頼できる証拠を発見したのだ。

その一方で、ロシアのプーチン大統領は「それはフェイクニュースだ」「ロシアを孤立させることは不可能だ」「ロシアはウクライナ東部の人々を救うために、ウクライナへの侵攻を避けることはできなかったのだ」と述べた。

4月上旬、ロシア軍はウクライナの東部や南東部に移動を開始した。彼らは当初キーウの征服をもくろんだ。しかし、ウクライナ軍の激しい抵抗にあい、また後方支援の問題もあって作戦を変更し、現在はウクライナ南東部の港町、マリウポリの制圧に注力しているところである。ロシア軍は、東部のドネツク州や、ルハンスク州の支配を狙っているが、他方、ウクライナ軍はロシア軍のミサイル巡洋艦、モスクワ号を撃沈するという華々しい戦果をあげたのである。

4月22日の時点では、ロシア軍はマリウポリをほぼ支配下に置き、ウクライナ軍が避難民とともに立てこもっている製鉄所を包囲している。プーチンは、第二次世界大戦で、ロシアがナチスドイツに勝利した記念日である5月9日には、ドネツク州とルハンスク州の占領を完了したい考えのようだ。

しかしながら、バイデン大統領は、ウクライナに対して8億ドルの追加軍事支援を発表し、EUもまた5億ユーロの支援を決定した。日本の岸田文雄首相は、ロシアの最大の銀行であるズベルスバンクの資産凍結や、ロシアからの石炭の輸入禁止、また駐日ロシア大使館の外交官の国外追放など、ロシアのウクライナ侵略に対する追加制裁を発表した。岸田首相は、「我々は非人道的な侵攻を止めさせ、平和的秩序を守る重大な岐路にいる」と述べたのである。

Russia's Invasion of Ukraine (3)
—How to prevent an abuse of power
（June 2022）

Nobody wants this war against Ukraine except for President Putin. It has been reported that even a local Russian assembly member has condemned this invasion since many young soldiers have died or been wounded. It's ridiculous! President Putin is a dictator, and this is Putin's war. Russia's invasion of Ukraine has no legitimacy. Putin explained that the aim of this war is to eliminate the neo- Nazi force in eastern Ukraine. However, this reason for the invasion is distorted. To unilaterally change the status-quo by force must not be forgiven.

Since April, Russian forces have focused on suppressing the eastern regions of Ukraine. On May 23, at the World Economic Forum's annual meeting (Davos forum), former U.S. Secretary of State Henry Kissinger, commented that it would be preferable to have the dividing line between Russia and Ukraine returned to the status-quo ante, before the Russian invasion in February. This means he recommends abandoning the recapture of the Crimean Peninsula, which Russia annexed in 2014.

Ukrainian President Zelenskyy strongly rebuffed this in a statement on May 25, saying "Those who advocate territorial partition are those who don't consider the Ukrainians living in the region." "Mr. Kissinger's calendar is not 2022, but 1938." He pointed out that Britain and France's appeasement policy toward a rising Nazi Germany supposedly led to the horrors of World War II.

The U.S. has supported Ukraine, bringing the total U.S. aid package to over 50 billion dollars. Specifically, military aid has been critical for Ukraine, which has angered Putin who has warned the U.S. of these actions.

146

ロシアのウクライナ侵略（3）
——如何にして権力の乱用を防ぐか
（2022年6月）

　誰一人としてウクライナに対するこの戦争を望んではいない。プーチン大統領を除いては。報道によると、ロシアのある地方議員でさえ、多くの若い兵士たちが亡くなり負傷しているという理由から、この戦争を非難したという。馬鹿げている！　プーチン大統領は独裁者であり、これはプーチンの戦争である。ロシアのウクライナ侵略には正当性が無い。プーチンは、この戦争の目的はウクライナ東部のネオナチ勢力を排除することであると説明している。しかしながら、この侵略の理由はこじつけだ。力による一方的な現状変更は、絶対に許されない。

　4月以来、ロシア軍は、ウクライナ東部を制圧することに注力してきた。5月23日、世界経済フォーラム（ダボス会議）では、元米国国務長官のヘンリー・キッシンジャー氏が、「2月のロシア侵略以前の状態に、ロシアとウクライナの分割線を設けることが望ましい」と提案した。これは、ロシアが2014年に併合したクリミア半島の奪還の放棄を勧めるものである。

　ウクライナのゼレンスキー大統領は、5月25日、この発表に強く反論して、「領土の分割を主張する人々は、地域に住むウクライナの人々のことを考えていない」「キッシンジャー氏のカレンダーは、2022年ではなく、1938年だ」と述べた。また大統領は、「大英帝国とフランスが、（当時）台頭するナチスドイツに対して宥和的な政策をとったことが、第二次世界大戦の悲劇につながったのだ」と指摘している。

　米国は、500億ドルを超える救援パッケージを提供して、ウクライ

On May 30, a spokesman from Ukraine's Ministry of Defense, reported that the battle in the Donbas region in the east has become extremely intense. Russian forces have focused attacks on the important city of Severodonetsk in Luhansk. Ukrainian forces are in a bad position.

According to Ukrainian media, "Russia is trying to attack deep into the Ukrainian defense line. Russian forces have entered central Severodonetsk and street fighting is taking place. The situation is still difficult."

However, President Biden announced on May 30, saying "The U.S. will not send rocket systems to Ukraine that can reach Russia." There were cautious opinions that Russia would likely start a large-scale counterattack.

As of June 14, Zelenskyy called on western nations to accelerate the supply of weapons to Ukraine, saying "We need long-range large weapons to battle the Russian forces." "If we don't get them, this war will be prolonged with further casualties."

This war is now at the crucial stage where Ukraine can shatter Putin's ambition to conquer Ukraine. The most difficult problem for politics is how to prevent an abuse of power by dictators. This applies not only to autocracies but also, to democracies. Modern politics needs to construct a system to control the despotism of power.

Russia's invasion of Ukraine left the town in ruins.

ナを支援している。とりわけ、ウクライナにとって軍事支援は極めて
重要である。しかしこのことが、軍事支援に関して米国に警告してき
たプーチンを怒らせた。

　5月30日には、ウクライナ防衛省の報道官が、東部ドンバス地方
での戦闘が非常に激しくなっていると発表した。ロシア軍は、ルハン
スク州の要衝セベロドネックに対して猛攻撃を加えており、ウクライ
ナ軍は劣勢に立たされている。

　ウクライナのメディアによると、「ロシアはウクライナの防衛ライ
ンを深く超えて攻撃を試みている。ロシア軍がセベロドネックの中心
部に入り込んで市街戦が起きており、（ウクライナ軍の）状況は依然
として厳しい」。

　にもかかわらず、バイデン大統領は5月30日、「米国はロシアに
届くようなロケットシステムをウクライナに提供することはない」と
述べたのである。ロシアが大規模な反撃を開始することを警戒する意
見があったからだ。

　6月14日の時点で、ゼレンスキー大統領は西側諸国に対して、兵
器の供給を加速するよう要求し、「我々はロシア軍と戦うための長距
離砲が必要だ。もしそれらが手に入らなければ、この戦争は長引き、
死傷者はさらに増えるだろう」と述べている。

　現在この戦争は、ウクライナを征服しようとするプーチン大統領の
野望を打ち砕くことができるかどうかの重要な段階にある。政治にと
って最も重要な問題は、如何にして独裁者による権力の乱用を防ぐか
ということにある。このことは、独裁政治だけではなく、民主主義体
制にもあてはまるものだ。現代政治は、権力の暴走をコントロールす
るシステムを構築する必要があるのだ。

Assassination of Former Prime Minister ABE Shinzo
（July 2022）

On July 8, 2022, shocking news suddenly appeared on my smartphone as I was on my way to Saitama prefecture to support a KOMEITO candidate for the House of Councillors election. At around 11:30 AM, former Prime Minister ABE Shinzo was shot in Nara City while making a stump speech.

ABE was pronounced dead at 5:03 PM. He was 67 years old. This news shook the nation and circled the globe. Prime Minister KISHIDA Fumio said, "I am deeply saddened and lost for words. We lost a great leader who loved the nation, looked to the future and made great achievements in various fields for the future of this country." He further added, "We must defend free and just elections, which are at the root of democracy. I will say this to the people until the very last moment of the campaign".

Police arrested the suspect YAMAGAMI Tetsuya, a 41-year-old man living in Nara City on suspicion of murder. This is the first time since World War Ⅱ that a former Prime Minister was assassinated by a firearm.

According to investigators, the mother of the suspect has been a member of the Family Federation for World Peace and Unification (Unification Church), and she donated around 100 million yen to the church. She joined the church around 1991 after her husband's suicide in 1984. As a consequence, the suspect's family fell into poverty and his mother went bankrupt. He had to give up on going to college. His uncle said, "His father had graduated from Kyoto University, and the son was extremely smart just like his father, but he had no choice but to work hard".

The suspect formerly entered the Maritime Self-Defense Force,

安倍晋三元首相の暗殺

（2022 年 7 月）

2022 年 7 月 8 日、参議院選挙の公明党の候補者を応援するため埼玉県に向かっていた時、突然私のスマートフォンに衝撃的なニュースが飛び込んできた。午前 11 時 30 分、奈良市で応援演説をしていた安倍晋三元首相が撃たれたのだ。

その後、安倍氏は同日午後 5 時 3 分に亡くなったと発表された。67 歳であった。このニュースは日本中を揺るがし、世界を駆け巡った。これを受けて、岸田首相は「深い悲しみに言葉がありません。私たちは、国家を愛し、未来を見つめ、この国の未来のために様々な分野で大きな功績を打ち立てた偉大な指導者を失いました」さらに、「私たちは、民主主義の根幹にある自由で公正な選挙を守らなければなりません。私は、このことを選挙の最後の最後まで訴えるつもりです」と述べた。

警察は、殺人の疑いで奈良市に住む 41 歳の男、山上徹也容疑者を逮捕した。元首相が小型銃で暗殺されたのは、戦後初めてのことである。捜査当局によると、容疑者の母親は「世界平和統一家庭連合（旧統一教会）」の一員であり、彼女は旧統一教会に約 1 億円もの寄付を行っていたという。彼女は、夫が 1984 年に自殺した後、1991 年頃に旧統一教会に入会している。その結果、容疑者の家族は貧困に陥り、母親は破産し、容疑者は大学に行くのを諦めなければならなかった。容疑者の叔父は「徹也の父親は京都大学を卒業し、その息子の徹也は父親に似て大変賢かったが、一生懸命働くしか無かったのだ」と答えている。

容疑者はかつて海上自衛隊に入隊していたのだが、2005 年に自殺

however he also attempted suicide in 2005, since hoping his brother and sister could benefit from a life insurance policy. He wanted to deal a blow to the church due to his grudge against it. Three years ago, he planned to attack the leader of the church with a firebomb while she was visiting Japan from South Korea. However, due to the novel coronavirus pandemic, the Unification Church leaders couldn't come to Japan. It was reported that the suspect was motivated to kill ABE after watching a video message sent by ABE to an affiliate of the Unification Church. He thought the church had close ties with ABE, and therefore, he changed his target to ABE from the leader of the church. Police said that he began making a gun from spring last year by researching how to make firearms, bullets and gunpowder online.

The late Mr. ABE Shinzo was the longest serving prime minister of Japan. His tenure in office was 8 years and 8 months. His economic policy package "Abenomics" consisted of three points; the first was a bold monetary easing policy by the Bank of Japan, second was an active fiscal policy, and third, a strategy of economic growth. It is true that "Abenomics" dramatically changed the economic condition of Japan. Owing to "Abenomics", the Japanese economy has been overcoming deflation. On the other hand, two consumption tax hikes in 2014 and 2019 resulted in a decline of "real wages", which curbed consumption. After his death, some people criticized that "Abenomics" turned out to be a failure, but it is only in hindsight. In order to break down the economic policies of the DPJ administration such as a strong yen, cheap stock prices, and fiscal reconstruction, a bold monetary easing policy and an active fiscal policy were indispensable and very effective. The novel coronavirus pandemic enabled us to be aware of strategies of economic growth such as digitalization, decarbonization and investment in human resources such as raising wages and child-rearing policy.

未遂を起こした。それは、彼の弟と妹を自分の生命保険で助けようと思ったからだった。容疑者は教会に対する恨みから、教会に対して打撃を加えようとした。3年前、教会の指導者が韓国から日本を訪問している間に、爆弾で攻撃しようと企てたのだ。しかし、新型コロナの世界的大流行のために、旧統一教会の指導者は日本に来ることができなかった。報道では、容疑者は旧統一教会の関連団体に対して送られた安倍元首相のビデオメッセージを見て、安倍氏を殺害しようと動機付けられたと伝えている。容疑者は、教会と安倍氏が緊密な関係にあると考え、そこで教会の指導者から安倍氏に狙いを変更したのだ。警察は、容疑者が昨年の春から、オンラインで小銃、弾丸や弾薬をどのようにして作るかを調べ、製造を始めたと述べている。

　故安倍晋三氏は、日本で最も長く首相を務めた。その在任期間は8年8カ月に及ぶ。彼の経済政策パッケージである「アベノミクス」は、3本の柱から構成されている。第1の柱は、日本銀行による大胆な金融緩和政策である。第2の柱は積極的財政であり、第3の柱は経済成長戦略である。「アベノミクス」が劇的に日本経済の状況を変えたことは確かである。「アベノミクス」のおかげで日本経済はデフレーションを克服しつつある。他方で、2014年と2019年の2回にわたる消費税の引き上げは、実質賃金の低下という結果をもたらし、消費を抑えることになった。安倍氏の死後、「アベノミクス」は失敗だったという人がいるが、それは後知恵に過ぎない。民主党政権時代の円高、株安、財政再建という経済政策を打破するには、「アベノミクス」の第1の大胆な金融緩和と、第2の積極財政政策は不可欠であり、またそれらは大変効果を発揮した。新型コロナウイルスの世界的大流行によって初めて、「デジタル化」や「脱炭素化」、また賃上げや子育て政策をはじめとする「人への投資」など、第3の経済成長戦略に気づくことになったのだ。

For foreign affairs, there was a pile of crucial and controversial agendas such as "Security Legislations" in terms of the right to collective self-defense and past conflicts between Japan and China. Nevertheless, the ABE administration had overcome these difficulties. In light of Chinese military expansion, the escalation of North Korea's missile launches, and Russia's invasion of Ukraine, "Security Legislations" led by the ABE administration turned out to be crucial for security surrounding Japan. It can be said that the "Free and Open Indo-Pacific" plan proposed by former Prime Minister ABE is the crucial cornerstone for the rule of law, economic prosperity and world peace.

ABE was a person of foresight. He must be one of the most consequential politicians around the world after World War II. After ABE stepped down, he soon became the leader of the LDP's largest faction, wielding significant influence over the party. He advocated that the government should increase the defense budget to 2% of gross domestic product. We can't foresee the effect of ABE's death.

In politics, we never know what tomorrow might bring. Politicians had better not depend too much on visible power, but instead pay attention to invisible powers such as public sentiment, social inequality and the unhappiness of the people. I would like to express my sincerest condolences on the loss of former Prime Minister ABE Shinzo.

Former Prime Minister ABE Shinzo and TAKEUCHI Yuzuru, Prime Minister's official residence.

　外交面では、集団的自衛権に関する「平和安全法制」や、日中間の
これまでの対立など、重要で論争のある課題が山積していた。しかし、
安倍政権はこれらの難題を克服していったのである。中国の軍事的拡
大、エスカレートする北朝鮮のミサイル発射、そしてロシアによるウ
クライナへの侵略などを踏まえると、安倍政権が主導した「平和安全
法制」は、日本の安全にとって不可欠であることが明らかとなった。
また、安倍元首相によって提唱された「自由で開かれたインド太平洋
構想」は、法の支配、経済的繁栄、そして世界平和のための極めて重
要な礎であると言えよう。

　安倍氏は先見性のある人物であった。彼は、第二次世界大戦以降で、
世界で最も功績を残した政治家の一人であるに違いない。彼は首相を
退任した後すぐに、自民党に大きな影響力を及ぼす最大派閥の領袖と
なり、政府は防衛予算をGDPの2%まで増やすべきだと唱導してい
た。安倍氏の死がどのような結果をもたらすかは予測できない。

　政治の世界は、一寸先は闇である。政治家は目に見える力に頼りす
ぎてはいけない。むしろ、民衆の感情や、社会的不平等、人々の不幸
など、目に見えない力を注視すべきである。元首相安倍晋三氏のご冥
福を衷心よりお祈り申し上げる。

安倍晋三元首相の殺害された翌日、
奈良に献花に訪れる人々
(2022年7月9日、写真＝Â©Rodrigo
Reyes Marin ／ ZUMA Press Wire ／
共同通信イメージズ)
People offering flowers at the crime
scene, Nara City, the day after the
assassination.

Victory for the 2022 House of Councillors Election
—The KOMEITO's Manifesto was evaluated as the Best
(August 2022)

In the House of Councillors election held July 10, just two days after the assassination of former Prime Minister ABE, the ruling coalition consisting of the LDP and KOMEITO, won a combined 76 (LDP 63; KOMEITO 13) of the 125 seats in the 248-member chamber. On the other hand, the opposition parties managed to obtain only 49 seats (CDP 17; JIP 12; NDP 5; JCP 4; Others 11). As a consequence, the ruling coalition parties secured a stable majority in both the House of Representatives and the House of Councillors for the next 3 years, so called a "Golden Three Years".

In the backdrop of this victory, there were several factors. First, the number of the novel coronavirus infections had declined during the election campaign. The approval rating for the Cabinet and the spread of the coronavirus infections tend to be in inverse proportion.

Second, due to Russia's invasion of Ukraine, many people keenly felt the need for political stability during uncertainty over security, energy supply and inflation.

Third, the ruling parties succeeded in separating between the National Democratic Party (NDP) from the other opposition parties. Before the election, the NDP's Chief Representative TAMAKI Yuichiro agreed to the 2022 government budget bill and started negotiations with the ruling parties regarding some designated policies.

Fourth, IZUMI Kenta, the Constitutional Democratic Party's (CDP) Chief Representative, initially advocated that the CDP should emphasize policy proposals rather than criticizing the government and ruling parties. However, in the ordinary Diet session, the CDP

2022 年参議院議員通常選挙の勝利
——公明党のマニフェストが第 1 位に
（2022 年 8 月）

　安倍前首相の暗殺から、わずか 2 日後の 7 月 10 日に行われた参議院選挙では、自民党と公明党の連立与党が、改選 125 議席（定数 248 議席）のうち、合計で 76 議席（自民党 63 議席、公明党 13 議席）を獲得した。一方、野党は 49 議席しか獲得できなかった（立憲民主党 17 議席、日本維新の会 12 議席、国民民主党 5 議席、日本共産党 4 議席、その他 11 議席）。その結果、連立与党は、衆議院と参議院の双方で安定した過半数を確保し、今後の 3 年間はいわゆる「黄金の 3 年間」となった。

　この勝利の背景には、いくつかの要因がある。第 1 に、新型コロナウイルスの感染者数が選挙戦中に減少したことだ。内閣の支持率と新型コロナウイルス感染拡大は反比例する傾向がある。

　第 2 に、ロシアのウクライナ侵攻により、多くの人々は安全保障、エネルギー供給、インフレに関する不確実性の中で、政治的安定の必要性を痛感したことだ。

　第 3 に、与党が、国民民主党と他の野党との分離に成功したことである。選挙に先立ち、国民民主党の玉木雄一郎代表は 2022 年予算案に賛成し、与党といくつかの政策について交渉を開始した。

　第 4 に、立憲民主党の泉健太代表は当初、「立憲民主党は、政府与党を批判するよりも、政策提言を重視すべきだ」と主張した。しかし、通常国会では立憲民主党が政策提言を行うことはほとんど無く、同党の支持率が低下したことだ。その結果、立憲民主党は実際の選挙で 6 議席を減らすことになった。

　第 5 に、野党は定数 1 の 32 選挙区で、互いに十分に協力すること

could hardly put forward any policy proposals, which led to the decline of the CDP's approval rating. As a result, the CDP actually reduced 6 seats in the election.

Fifth, the opposition parties couldn't cooperate sufficiently with each other in 32 single seat constituencies. Before the election, they were only able to integrate their candidates in 11 districts, which led to an LDP victory in 28 single seat constituencies.

Sixth, according to the analysis of public opinion polls, it seems that the assassination of former Prime Minister ABE worked in favor of the LDP.

That is why the LDP secured 63 seats, increasing 8 seats. The KOMEITO won 7 seats in 7 constituencies and 6 seats in proportional representation, securing 6.18 million votes in total.

The Waseda University Manifesto Research Institution (WUMRI) evaluated the KOMEITO's Manifesto as the best Manifesto of all political parties for the 2022 Upper House election. I suppose that the WUMRI highly appreciated the KOMEITO's Manifesto considering its purpose, consistency, probability and innovation. This led to victories of the KOMEITO in undecided constituencies.

The aim of our Manifesto is to construct a social-economic system that people can really experience happiness by correcting various issues brought on by capitalism such as disparity and poverty, and serious climate change. The KOMEITO pledged six major policies; First was to enhance economic growth leading to an increase of employment and income levels. This includes energy security, decarbonization and digitalization. Second was to construct a society that every generation can support each other through the social security system. Specifically, we put an emphasize on child-rearing and education in light of the declining birth rate. Third was to bolster defense capabilities for the deteriorating security environment surrounding Japan. Fourth was to develop an abundant local region through digitalization.

ができなかった。選挙前には、11 選挙区でしか候補者を統合できず、これが定数 1 の 28 選挙区での自民党勝利を許すことになった。

第 6 に、世論調査の分析によると、安倍元首相の暗殺は自民党に有利に働いたようだ。

このような理由から自民党は 8 議席増の 63 議席を獲得。公明党は 7 選挙区で 7 議席の全員当選、比例代表では 6 議席を確保、618 万票を獲得した。

早稲田大学マニフェスト研究所は、2022 年の参議院選挙において、全政党のマニフェストの中で公明党のマニフェストを第 1 位に評価した。同研究所は、公明党のマニフェストの目的、一貫性、実現可能性や先進性などを考慮して高く評価したものと思われる。これが激戦区での公明党の勝利につながっている。

我々のマニフェストの目的は、格差や貧困、深刻な気候変動など資本主義によってもたらされた様々な問題を是正することによって、人々が真に幸福を実感できる社会経済システムの構築することにある。

その上で、公明党は、6 つの主要政策を公約した。第 1 に、経済成長を高め、雇用と所得を拡大すること。これにはエネルギー安全保障、脱炭素化とデジタル化を含んでいる。第 2 に、社会保障システムを通じて、全ての世代が互いに支え合う社会を構築すること。とりわけ、少子社会を踏まえて子育てと教育に重点を置いた。第 3 に、日本を取り巻く安全保障環境の悪化を背景として、防衛能力を強化すること。第 4 に、デジタル化で豊かな地域社会を開拓すること。第 5 に、感染症の大流行から国民の命と健康を守ること。第 6 に、地球温暖化によってもたらされる巨大災害への対策を強化することである。

野党の中では、日本維新の会のみが 6 議席を増加。日本共産党は、その綱領の中で、自衛隊の解散と日米同盟の廃棄を主張していることから、2 議席を失うこととなった。

Fifth, to protect people's lives and health from infectious pandemics. Sixth was to strengthen countermeasures against disasters brought on by the global warming.

Among the opposition parties, only the JIP (Japan Innovation Party) increased 6 seats. The JCP (Japan Communist Party) lost 2 seats due to its platform of advocating the dissolution of the Self Defense Force and the abolition of the Japan - U.S. Alliance.

After the election, the seventh wave of coronavirus infections (BA.5) has been surging and as of July 28, the number of confirmed cases per day reached 233,000, the highest ever. However, the KISHIDA Cabinet has no intension to impose restrictions on economic and social activities for the time being, since there are less people in serious condition under the Omicron variant, BA.5. However, as I anticipated, the approval rating of the KISHIDA Cabinet has started to decline.

The KOMEITO's Manifesto for the 2022 House of Councillors Election.

　選挙後、コロナウイルス感染の第 7 波（BA.5）が急増しており、7月 28 日時点で確認された症例数は、1 日当たり過去最多の 233,000人に達した。 しかし、岸田内閣は、オミクロン変異種、BA.5 の下では、重篤な状態にある人が少ないことを踏まえ、当面、経済・社会活動に制限を課すつもりはない。しかし、私が予想していた通り、岸田内閣の支持率が低下し始めたのである。

参議院選挙の応援演説（2022 年 7 月 4 日、福岡県）
The campaign speech for the House of Councillors Election, Fukuoka
Prefecture, July 4, 2022.

National Security of Japan

(September 2022)

The U.S. Speaker of the House of Representatives, Nancy Pelosi, visited Taiwan and met with Taiwanese President Tsai on August 2 and 3 despite fierce warnings from China.

Pelosi said to Tsai, "America's determination to preserve democracy here in Taiwan and around the world remains ironclad." Tsai responded, "We will strengthen our national defense capabilities and strive for peace and stability in the Taiwan Strait".

Before Pelosi's visit to Taiwan, Chinese President Xi Jinping had conveyed his firm opposition to the perceived interference in the Taiwan issue, stating, "Those who play with fire will perish by it." Soon after U.S. Speaker Pelosi left Taiwan, China conducted large-scale military exercises around Taiwan, including firing five missiles that landed in Japan's exclusive economic zone (EEZ) for the first time. "This is extremely irresponsible and a significant escalation of tensions." Defense Minister KISHI Nobuo announced in a news conference, "We strongly condemn this grave matter involving Japan's national security and the safety of its people".

Mainland China has clarified its firm intention to unite Taiwan sooner or later. U.S. President Biden does not voice an objection to China's position that mainland China and Taiwan are inseparable; however, he showed his intention to adhere to the U.S.'s "One China" policy which is also involved in the security of Taiwan.

The U.S. hasn't directly interfered with the invasion of Ukraine by Russia, since Ukraine doesn't belong to NATO. However, under the U.S. "One China" policy, it is ambiguous whether the U.S. could really get involved in the event of a Taiwan contingency.

In a Taiwan Strait emergency, Japan must first judge the

日本の国家安全保障

（2022 年 9 月）

　米国下院議長のナンシー・ペロシ氏は、中国からの激しい警告にもかかわらず、8 月 2 日と 3 日にかけて台湾を訪問し、蔡総統と会談した。

　ペロシ米下院議長は蔡総統に、「ここ台湾と世界中で民主主義を維持するというアメリカの決意は揺るぎない」と述べたが、これに対し蔡総統は「国防力を強化し、台湾海峡の平和と安定のために努力する」と答えた。

　ペロシ米下院議長の台湾訪問の前に、中国の習近平国家主席は、台湾問題への明らかな干渉に断固反対を表明し、「火で遊ぶ者はそれによって滅びるだろう」と述べていた。 ペロシ米下院議長が台湾を離れた直後、中国は台湾周辺での大規模な軍事演習を実施し、その中で初めて日本の排他的経済水域（EEZ）に 5 発のミサイルを発射着弾させたのである。「これは極めて無責任であり、緊張の重大なエスカレーションだ」。岸信夫防衛相は記者会見で、「日本の国家安全保障と国民の安全に関わるこの重大な問題を強く非難する」と表明した。

　中国本土は、遅かれ早かれ台湾を統一するという確固たる意思を明確にしている。バイデン米大統領は、中国本土と台湾は不可分であるという中国の立場に異議を唱えてはいない。しかし一方で、彼は米国の「一つの中国」政策は、台湾の安全保障にも関わるという意志を示しているのである。

　ウクライナは NATO に所属していないので、米国はロシアによるウクライナ侵略に直接介入はしていない。しかし、米国の「一つの中国」政策の下では、台湾の不測の事態に米国が本当に軍事関与できる

situation in light of peace and security laws, which classify a contingency into 3 categories: an armed attack on Japan, a threat to the national existence of Japan, and a significant impact on Japan. In accordance with these categories, Japan needs to take different countermeasures.

On May 24, six Chinese and Russian bombers flew together around Japan. This was a military demonstration against Japan, the host nation of the Quad which is a four-country framework including Japan, the U.S., Australia and India. Any of those bombers are capable of carrying nuclear weapons. Defense Minister KISHI said, "We have to be seriously concerned from a security perspective", and criticized China for acting together with Russia, the aggressor nation.

North Korea has also been escalating all ranges of missile launches. On May 26, 2022, the UN Security Council rejected a draft resolution to impose additional sanctions on North Korea over its ballistic missile launches, since Russia and China vetoed the resolution.

As I have explained, the security environment surrounding Japan has further deteriorated. The LDP claim that th

e government needs to increase the defense budget to 2% of the gross domestic product (GDP). The KOMEITO agrees in strengthening the capability of defense; however, advocates that the defense budget should be drawn up by reviewing what is really needed for security, and not with a predetermined 2% of the GDP. This will be the biggest issue in the extraordinary Diet.

UPDATE: On December 8, 2022, Prime Minister KISHIDA and the ruling bloc, the LDP and KOMEITO agreed to secure about ¥43 trillion for defense spending over 5 years from fiscal 2023. In fiscal 2027, the defense budget including supplementary projects will

かどうかは曖昧である。

　台湾海峡の有事においては、我が国はまず、平和安全法制に照らして、日本に対する「武力攻撃事態」、日本の「存立危機事態」、日本への「重要影響事態」のいずれの分類に該当するかを判断しなければならない。これらの分類に応じて、日本は異なる対策を講じる必要がある。

　5月24日、中国とロシアの爆撃機6機が一緒に日本周辺を飛び回った。これは、日本、米国、オーストラリア、インドの4カ国の枠組みであるクワッド（Quad）の主催国である日本に対する軍事的威圧である。これらの爆撃機はいずれも核兵器を搭載することができる。岸防衛大臣は「安全保障の観点から真剣に懸念しなければならない」と述べ、侵略国ロシアと共に行動する中国を批判した。

　北朝鮮はまた、あらゆる範囲のミサイル発射をエスカレートさせている。2022年5月26日、国連安保理では、北朝鮮の弾道ミサイル発射をめぐって追加制裁を課す決議案が、ロシアと中国が拒否権を発動したため否決された。

　このように、日本を取り巻く安全保障環境はさらに悪化している。自民党は、日本政府に対して、防衛予算をGDP比2%にまで増やす必要があると要求している。公明党は防衛能力を強化することには同意をしている。しかし「防衛予算は、はじめにGDP比2%ありきではなく、日本の安全保障のために本当に必要なものは何かを検証することによって策定すべきである」というのが公明党の主張である。この問題は臨時国会の最大の課題となるであろう。

（後日談）

　2022年12月8日、岸田首相と連立与党の自民党、公明党は、2023年度から5年間の防衛費の総額を43兆円とすることで合意した。2027

reach around ¥9 trillion, equivalent to 2% of the GDP in fiscal 2022.

Moreover, the revised National Security Strategy (NSS) acquires a so-called counterstrike capability, allowing Japan to strike targets in enemy territory to deter attacks. It is interpreted that counterstrike capability is originally within the scope of Constitution so long as three conditions are applied: 1) that an armed attack has occurred; 2) that there is no other way to halt an attack; and 3) that the use of force is limited to the minimum needed. However, in light of Japan's exclusively defense-oriented posture, the U.S. military force has been allowed to exercise it, while the roll of the Self Defense Force (SDF) has been limited to intercept missiles from enemy. The KISHIDA administration decided to bolster a power of deterrence by allowing the SDF to exercise counterstrike capabilities. It's needless to say that preemptive strikes are not permitted.

Escort vessel Maya (Japan Maritime Self-Defense Force, Website)

年の防衛費は補足的な事業を含めて約9兆円となり、これは2022年の国内総生産（GDP）の2%に相当する。

　また、今回改定された「国家安全保障戦略」では、いわゆる日本の「反撃能力」を求めており、これは敵の攻撃を抑止するため敵の領土の目標に反撃することを認めるものである。本来「反撃能力」は、3つの条件が当てはまる限りにおいて、憲法の範囲内であると解釈されている。その3条件とは、（1）他国からの武力攻撃が発生したこと。（2）他にとりうる手段が無いこと。（3）日本の武力行使は必要最小限であることである。しかしながら、専守防衛の姿勢から、これまでは米軍がこれを担い、自衛隊の役割は敵からのミサイルを迎撃することに限定されていた。岸田政権は、自衛隊に「反撃能力」の行使を認めることによって、抑止力を強化することを決定した。先制攻撃が許されないことは言うまでもない。

PAC-3 (Japan Air Self-Defense Force, Website)

A Rapidly Aging Society with Fewer Children
—"Child-Rearing Support Master Plan" by the KOMEITO
(November 2022)

In 2022, the number of babies born in Japan will drop below 800 thousand for the first time since the end of World War II. The birth rate in 2021 is 1.30, and if this level continues, the population of Japan will gradually decline and dip below 100 million people by 2053. (Currently, 128 million) On the other hand, Japan's society is rapidly aging. In 2021, those over 65 years old was 28.9%, or around 36 million people, and those over 75 years of age was 14.9%, or around 19 million people.

In a quickly aging society with fewer children, Japan will be deprived of its vitality, which will lead to a decline in industry, and the unsustainability of the medical care system, elderly care, and pension systems. In particular, the government expenditure for social security has been expanding and has reached around 36 trillion yen for 2021, while tax revenues account for about 60 trillion yen.

As a consequence, an aging society has imposed tremendous pressure to government finances. In order to secure sources of revenue, the ABE administration raised the consumption tax rate from 5% to 10% over the last five years. This has enabled the government to secure 14 trillion yen in tax revenues. However, despite the tax hike, the government expenditure for social security will further increase year on year, due to the rapidly aging society.

For the countermeasures against the declining birth rate, the ABE administration approved free education for children (3-5 years), as well as for private senior high school students and university students whose parents are classified as low income.

加速する少子高齢化社会
—— 「子育て応援トータルプラン」公明党が発表
（2022 年 11 月）

　2022 年、日本の出生数は戦後初めて 80 万人を下回る見込みだ。2021 年の合計特殊出生率は 1.30 であり、もしもこの水準が続くならば、日本の人口は次第に減少していき、2053 年には 1 億人を下回ることになるだろう。その一方で、日本の社会は急速に高齢化している。2021 年の 65 歳以上の割合は 28.9%、約 3,600 万人であり、75 歳以上の割合は 14.9%、約 1,900 万人となっている。

　急速に進む少子高齢化社会の中で、日本はその活力を奪われていくことになるが、このことは産業の衰退や医療、介護、年金制度の不安定さにつながっていくだろう。特に、社会保障のための政府支出は拡大の一途であり、2021 年には約 36 兆円に達しているが、他方で税収入は約 60 兆円となっている。

　その結果、高齢化社会は政府財政にとてつもない圧力をかけている。その財源を確保するために、安倍政権はこの 5 年間で消費税率を 5%から 10% まで引き上げた。このおかげで、政府は年間 14 兆円もの税収を確保することができたのである。しかし、この税率引き上げにもかかわらず、社会保障のための政府支出は、社会が急速に高齢化していくことから、毎年さらに増えていくだろう。

　低下していく出生率に対する政策として、安倍政権は 3 歳児から 5 歳児までの保育料の無償化とともに、私立高校の授業料や、低収入と認定された家庭の大学生の授業料の無償化を認めた。日本では、小学校から中学校までは義務教育であり、また公立高校は 2011 年から無償化となっている。

　政府は、少子化の原因について、経済、働き方、親への支援など

Elementary school to junior high school is compulsory in Japan, and public senior high schools have been free since 2011.

The government has to research the causes of the declining of birth rate from various viewpoints such as economy, working styles, parental support, and so forth. Generally speaking, it is said that the sluggish growth of real wages, shortages in nursery schools and teachers, an increase in female workers with advanced academic backgrounds getting married later in life, heavy burdens for education, and so on. These issues need to be addressed, not only by the government, but also by the private sector to create a society where younger generations can get married and have children.

In November, 2022, in light of a rapidly aging society with fewer children, the KOMEITO released the "Child-Rearing Support Master Plan" to aid child-rearing and education, which I formulated as the policy chief. This plan aims to prioritize the happiness of children and proposes concrete measures such as reducing the burdens on parents from pregnancy to college graduate, dissolution of inequality between males and females, economic aid for young people and a better work-life balance. It needs over 6 trillion yen to be realized. The fundamental issue for Japan is the declining birth rate, and we do want to realize this "Child-Rearing Support Master Plan".

The KOMEITO released the "Child-Rearing Support Master Plan", November, 2022.

様々な観点から調査しなければならない。一般的には、実質賃金のわずかばかりの増加、保育園や保育士の不足、高学歴で晩婚化する女性労働者の増加、教育費の重い負担などが指摘されている。この問題には、政府だけではなく民間セクターにおいても、若い世代が結婚して、子どもを持てる社会を創るために取り組む必要があるだろう。

　2022年11月、加速する少子高齢化社会を踏まえて、公明党は、子育てと教育をサポートするための「子育て応援トータルプラン」を発表した。これは私が政務調査会長として策定を主導したものだ。本プランは、子どもの幸福を最優先にすることを目的として、妊娠から大学卒業までの親の負担軽減や、男女不平等の解消、若い人々に対する経済支援、またワークライフバランスなど具体的な対策を提示している。これらを実現するには6兆円を超える財源が必要となる。日本の根本的な課題は少子化であり、この「子育て応援トータルプラン」を是非とも実現していきたい。

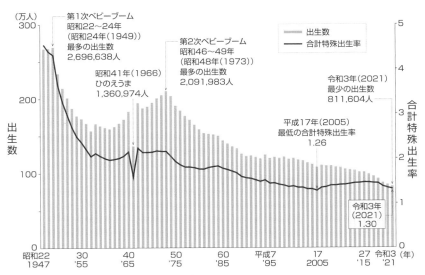

出生数および合計特殊出生率の年次推移
注：昭和47年以前は沖縄県を含まない。　出所：厚生労働省「人口動態統計」

Complete Solution for the North Korea Abduction Issue
(December 2022)

On October 4, North Korea launched a ballistic missile which flew over northern Japan and landed in the Pacific Ocean. The missile flew about 4,600 kilometers with a maximum altitude of 970 kilometers. As of December 19, Pyongyang has launched at least 66 missiles this year alone. These outrageous acts are part of a clear escalation by the isolated nation.

We should be careful in regards to security for the Korean Peninsula and never fail in making North Korea abandon their nuclear weapons and various range missiles. This includes finding a complete solution for the North Korea abduction issue.

On November 15, 1977, Megumi Yokota, a girl of thirteen and a junior high school student, was abducted by North Korea on her way home from school in Niigata Prefecture. At first, the Japanese police couldn't identify the real culprit, but in 1997, the Japanese government recognized 10 abductees taken (now 17) by North Korea. These are unprecedented crimes that violated Japan's sovereignty and human rights. These crimes should never be forgiven. It's needless to say that the past colonial rule of the Korean Peninsula by the Empire of Japan from 1910 to 1945 has nothing to do with this issue.

In 2002, former Prime Minister KOIZUMI Junichiro of the LDP-KOMEITO ruling coalition, penetrated Pyongyang and negotiated with Kim Jong-il on this issue. As a consequence, Kim recognized the abductions by North Korea and apologized. However, this resulted in the return of only five abductees to Japan. North Korea claimed that the rest of the abductees, including Megumi Yokota, had died. However, the ashes that North Korea provided

北朝鮮による拉致問題の完全解決を

（2022 年 12 月）

　10 月 4 日、北朝鮮は高度 970km、距離 4,600km に及ぶ弾道ミサイルを北日本を飛び越えて太平洋に打ち込んだ。12 月 19 日で、北朝鮮は今年だけで少なくとも 66 発のミサイルを発射している。これらの暴挙は孤立した国家の明白なエスカレーションの一環であり、その苦境を示している。

　我々は、朝鮮半島の安全保障に警戒を払うべきであり、北朝鮮に必ず核兵器と様々な種類のミサイルを放棄させなければならない。このことは、北朝鮮による（日本人）拉致問題の解決を見出すことを含むものである。

　1977 年 11 月 15 日、新潟県の 13 歳の中学生であった横田めぐみさんは、学校からの帰り道で北朝鮮によって拉致された。最初のうち、日本の警察は真の容疑者を特定することができなかったが、1997 年になって日本政府は、北朝鮮によって拉致された 10 名の被害者を認定した（現在は 17 名）。これは、日本の主権と人権を侵害する前代未聞の事件である。このような犯罪は決して許されることではない。言うまでもないが、この事件は 1910 年から 1945 年までの大日本帝国による朝鮮半島の植民地支配とは何の関係も無い。

　2002 年、自公連立政権の小泉純一郎首相が平壌に乗り込み、この問題について金正日と交渉した。その結果、金正日は北朝鮮による拉致を認め謝罪したのである。しかしながら、日本に戻るのは 5 人の被害者のみとなった。北朝鮮は、横田めぐみさんを含めてその他の被害者は死亡したと主張。ところが、北朝鮮が証拠として提供した遺骨は、DNA 鑑定によって偽物であることが判明したのだ。彼らは

as evidence turned out to be counterfeit through DNA analysis. Therefore, they must still remain in North Korea. North Korea must promptly return all abductees to Japan without any conditions. Nevertheless, North Korea claims the abduction issue has already been resolved.

I am also chairperson of the North Korea abduction issue commission of the KOMEITO party. The resolution of this issue is especially important for Japan and is a prerequisite condition for normalizing the relationship between Japan and North Korea. The Japanese government has strongly pressured North Korea for the resolution of the abduction issue by imposing economic sanctions together with international societies.

The United Nations released a report February 2014 that abductions by North Korea occurred in many countries such as South Korea, Thailand, Malaysia, Singapore, France, Italy, Netherlands, and so on. The UN demanded North Korea to resolve these issues as soon as possible. Besides, it is crucial for the Japanese people to express their strong determination to get all abductees back to Japan immediately.

The national convention, pursuing a complete solution for the North Korea abduction issue, Tokyo.

未だに北朝鮮に残っているに違いない。北朝鮮は、直ちにすべての被害者を無条件で日本に帰さなければならない。にもかかわらず北朝鮮は、拉致問題はすでに解決ずみだと主張しているのである。

　私は、公明党拉致問題対策委員長でもある。この問題の解決は日本にとって特に重要であり、日本と北朝鮮の国交正常化の前提条件となっている。日本政府は国際社会と連携し、北朝鮮に対する経済制裁を課すことによって、北朝鮮が拉致問題の解決に向けて前進するよう強く要求してきた。

　国連は 2014 年 2 月に、北朝鮮による拉致問題が、韓国、タイ、マレーシア、シンガポール、フランス、イタリア、オランダなど世界の多くの国々で起こっていることを報告しており、北朝鮮に対してできるだけ早期にこの問題を解決するよう迫っている。加えて、日本の人々が、すべての拉致被害者を直ちに取り戻す強い決意を表明することが、極めて重要なのである。

全拉致被害者の即時一括帰国を求める国民大集会（東京）

Epilogue
Turbulent Times for Japanese Politics
(December 2022)

Mikhail Gorbachev, the final leader and only president of the former Soviet Union died on August 30, 2022. He was a one-of-a kind statesman who changed the course of history, and played a crucial role in ending the Cold War and pulling down the Iron Curtain. Putin should have learned from Gorbachev.

Ukraine's President Zelenskyy announced on September 11 that areas in the northeast Kharkiv province had been freed. The Ukraine military has been gaining momentum towards taking back territory in the east. It was reported that Ukraine had recaptured over 3,000 square kilometers of land. The Russian side had already recognized its withdrawal, and ordered the retreat from the western bank of the Dnieper River in the southern Kherson province on November 9, which highlights Russia's predicament. However, Russian military began counterattacks using missiles against Ukrainian infrastructure facilities, such as power and water supplies. Furthermore, western nations are concerned by the threat of nuclear weapons by Russia. International societies need to unite to cease Russia's invasion of Ukraine as soon as possible. To end Russia's invasion of Ukraine depends on its "dictator", President Putin, and ultimately, on the Russian people.

Regarding East Asia, U.S. President Joe Biden stated clearly that its military would defend Taiwan if China attacked the island in an interview with CBS on September 18. This statement could be perceived as a revision of the "Ambiguous Strategy" of previous administrations that did not clarify a response in the contingency of the Taiwan Strait. On the other hand, on October 16, Chinese Communist Party General Secretary Xi Jinping stated at the party

エピローグ
激動 日本の政治
（2022 年 12 月）

　旧ソ連邦の最後の指導者で、唯一の大統領であったミハイル・ゴルバチョフ氏が、2022 年の 8 月 30 日に亡くなった。彼は、歴史を変えた唯一無二の政治家であり、冷戦を終結させ、鉄のカーテンを下ろすにあたって決定的な役割を果たした。プーチン氏はゴルバチョフ氏から学ぶべきであった。

　ウクライナのゼレンスキー大統領は、9 月 11 日、「北東部ハルキウ州の地域を解放した」と発表した。ウクライナ軍は東部の領土奪還に向けて、勢いを増している。ウクライナは、3,000㎢の領土を取り戻したと伝えられている。ロシア側はすでに撤退を認めており、また 11 月 9 日には、南部ヘルソン州のドニプロ川西岸からの退却を命じた。これらはロシアの苦境を示すものだ。しかしながら、ロシア軍はウクライナの電力や水道など、インフラ施設へのミサイル攻撃を開始した。さらに西側諸国は、ロシアによる核兵器使用の脅威を懸念している。国際社会は、一致団結して一刻も早くロシアによるウクライナ侵略を停止させる必要がある。この侵略を終わらせることは、一人の独裁者、プーチン大統領次第だが、究極的にはロシア国民にかかっている。

　東アジアに関して、米国大統領のジョー・バイデン氏は 9 月 18 日、「もしも中国が台湾を攻撃したならば、米軍は台湾を守る」と、CBS テレビのインタビューで明確に述べた。この表明は、これまで台湾有事の際の対応を明確にしていなかった歴代政権の「曖昧戦略」を変更するものと受け取られる可能性がある。一方で、10 月 16 日、中国共産党総書記の習近平氏は、全国人民代表会議で「中国の

congress that China would not hesitate to use force to reunify Taiwan, which is a core profit for the mainland. On October 23, Xi unveiled a new leadership team fortified with loyalists to consolidate his power in a precedent-busting third term. However, to unilaterally change the status-quo by force must not be forgiven. We hope for a peaceful resolution of the Taiwan issue.

The World Health Organization (WHO)'s Director-General Tedros said on September 14 that the end is in sight for the pandemic caused by COVID-19. According to researchers from Oxford University in the UK, more than 600 million people around the world have been infected so far, with 6.5 million deaths.

As of December 2022, three years have passed since the outbreak of the novel coronavirus infection, which first come to Japan in January 2020. The world has suffered from COVID-19 and a serious economic depression. Russia's invasion of Ukraine has created both a global security and energy crisis, which has accelerated inflation.

However, Japanese society has been overcoming the coronavirus pandemic by promoting vaccinations from Pfizer or Moderna and getting through the depression by proactive fiscal policies, leading to the recovery of the GDP and tax revenue. This proves the accuracy of our proactive fiscal policies. The government currently puts an emphasis on countermeasures against inflation such as energy costs.

The coronavirus pandemic revealed the delay in digitalization in Japanese society. Through the 2021 general election and the 2022 House of Councillors election, the KOMEITO pledged to promote the "My Number card" which plays an important part as infrastructure for digitalization by granting points worth up to 30,000 yen to those who get the card. (We had initially planned 100,000 points, but later altered this since an allowance of 100,000

核心的利益である台湾を統一するためには武力の行使もためらわない」と述べた。10月23日には、習近平氏は慣例を破る3期目に入り、彼の権力を強化するために側近で固められた新たな指導部を明らかにした。しかしながら、現状を力によって一方的に変更することは、断じて許されない。我々は台湾問題の平和的解決を望んでいる。

　世界保健機関（WHO）のテドロス事務局長は、9月14日、「コロナウイルスによって引き起こされたパンデミック（世界的大流行）は、収束が視野に入ってきた」と述べた。英国のオックスフォード大学の研究者たちによるプロジェクトによると、これまでに世界中で6億人以上が感染し、650万人が死亡したとされている。

　2022年12月時点で、日本で2020年1月に新型コロナウイルス感染が発生してから3年が経った。世界は新型コロナと深刻な経済不況に苦しんできた。ロシアによるウクライナ侵略は、世界の安全保障とエネルギーの危機を生み出し、インフレーションを加速させている。

　しかしながら、日本社会はファイザーやモデルナのワクチン接種を促進することによって、コロナウイルスのパンデミックを克服しつつあり、また積極的な財政政策で不況を乗り切り、それが国内総生産（GDP）や税収の回復につながっている。これは、我々の積極財政政策が正しかったことを証明している。政府は今、エネルギーコスト対策などインフレーション対策に重点を置いているところだ。

　コロナウイルスのパンデミックは、日本社会のデジタル化の遅れを暴露した。そこで公明党は、2021年の衆議院総選挙と2022年の参議院選挙を通じて、「デジタル化の基盤として重要な役割を果たすマイナンバーカードの普及」を公約に掲げ、その際カード取得者には、最大で30,000円相当のポイントを付与することとした。（我々は当初10万ポイントを計画していたが、衆院選の公約として、0～

179

yen to children aged 0-18 was adopted as the 2021 general election pledge. After the 2021 general election, 20,000 points were decided through the negotiation between the LDP and KOMEITO.) As a consequence, the number of applicants for the card has soared from 35 million (27%) to over 83 million (67%) for the past two years. It will reach around 100 million in the near future. The "My Number card" has a firm system in place to prevent cyberattacks and leaks of the publics information. The promotion of the "My Number card" is sure to generate large sources of revenue by urging administrative reform and streamlining social security. It will also prompt further digitalization for society, leading to improvements in productivity, raising wages and economic growth.

Mr. SAITO Tetsuo, Secretary-General of the KOMEITO at that time, insisted on a "Carbon Neutral Society in 2050" in the plenary session of the House of Representatives in January 2020. The KOMEITO is the only political party to propose a "Carbon Neutral Society in 2050" in the Diet. Prime Minister SUGA, who took office in September, agreed with this proposal and announced it as an international pledge. In order to implement this pledge, he decided to reduce greenhouse gases by 46% by 2030, compared to levels from 2013. However, it was not easy to achieve this ambitious target. So, I proposed to Prime Minister SUGA in the budget committee of the 2020 extraordinary Diet session in the fall that the government should set up a large scale fund totaling ¥ 15 trillion for developing innovative technologies such as storage batteries, the use of hydrogen, carbon dioxide capture, utilization and storage. Soon after, SUGA accepted these proposals and established the "Green Innovation Fund" totaling 2 trillion yen. This fund will develop new energy sources instead of relying on fossil fuels, and contribute to decarbonization, energy security and the creation of new industries and jobs.

Investment in human resources is a crucial policy for the

18歳の子どもたちに10万円を給付することを決定したので、ポイントは変更することになった。選挙後、自民党や財務省との交渉で20,000ポイントとなったが）その結果、カードの申請者数はこの2年間で3,400万人（27%）から8,300万人（67%）を超えるまでに急増している。まもなく1億人に達すると思われる。マイナンバーカードは、サイバー攻撃や情報の流出を防ぐ強固なシステムを有している。カードの普及は、行政改革や社会保障の効率化を促し、大きな財源を生み出すに違いない。また、社会のデジタル化を促進し、生産性を高め、賃金を引き上げ、経済成長をもたらすことになるだろう。

　公明党の斉藤鉄夫幹事長（当時）は、2020年1月の衆議院本会議代表質問で「2050年脱炭素社会」の実現を訴えた。公明党は国会で「2050年脱炭素化社会実現」を提案した唯一の政党である。9月に就任した菅首相はこの提案に賛同し、国際公約として表明するとともに、この公約を具体化するために「2030年までに、2013年と比べて温室効果ガスを46%削減すること」を決定したのである。しかし、この野心的な目標の達成は容易では無い。そこで、私は2020年秋の臨時国会の予算委員会で、菅首相に対して、「政府が15兆円に及ぶ大規模な基金を創り、蓄電池、水素の利用、二酸化炭素の回収・利用・貯留などの革新的な技術を発展させるべきだ」と提案した。菅首相は、直ちにこの提案を受け入れて、2兆円規模の「グリーン・イノベーション基金」を創設したのである。この基金は、化石燃料に代わる新しいエネルギーを開発し、脱炭素化・エネルギー安全保障、そして新産業と雇用の創出に貢献するであろう。

　人への投資は、日本経済のイノベーションにとって、デジタル化や脱炭素化と並ぶ極めて重要な政策であり、これには労働者に対するより高い賃金の分配と、子育てや教育への支援が含まれている。公明党は、2022年の参議院選挙では、「労使双方から選ばれた経済学者から

innovation of the Japanese economy as well as digitalization and decarbonization. This includes the distribution of higher wages and support for child-rearing and education. The KOMEITO proposed in the 2022 House of Councillors election that the government should set up the "Third Committee" which consists of economic scholars elected by labor and management to indicate the target for raising wages in the spring labor-management negotiations. Continuous raising wages will make it possible to overcome inflation and to reconstruct Japanese finances. Furthermore, I think that the Bank of Japan should announce a policy that commits itself to raising wages as well as inflation targets.

The most important investment in human resources is to support child-rearing and education. On November 8, 2022, the KOMEITO released the "Child-Rearing Support Master Plan" to aid child-rearing and education, which I formulated as the policy chief through the research and deliberation over the period of two years. This plan aims to prioritize the happiness of children by proposing concrete measures such as reducing or eliminating the burdens on parents from pregnancy to college graduation, dissolution of inequality between males and females, economic aid for young people and a better work-life balance. It needs over 6 trillion yen to be realized. The fundamental issue for Japan is the declining birth rate, and we do want to realize this "Child-Rearing Support Master Plan". Currently, Prime Minister KISHIDA has come to be aware of the importance of this matter and stated that the government will implement an unprecedented child-rearing policy such as an expansion of child allowances and benefits of ¥ 100,000 to all children aged 0-2 every year based on the "Child-Rearing Support Master Plan" of the KOMEITO.

I resigned as Chairperson of the Policy Research Council of the

なる『第三者委員会』を創設し、春闘の労使交渉において賃金引き上げの目安を提示すべきだと」提案した。継続的な賃上げは、インフレーションの克服と日本財政の再建を可能にするだろう。さらに、私は日本銀行が物価目標だけではなく、賃上げにも関与する政策を表明すべきだと考えている。

　最も重要な人への投資は、「子育てと教育に対する支援」である。公明党は、2022年11月8日、子育てと教育支援のための「子育て応援トータルプラン」を発表した。これは私が政務調査会長として、2年に及ぶ調査と議論を経てとりまとめまとめたものだ。このプランでは、子どもの幸福を最優先として、妊娠から大学卒業までの親の負担の軽減や無償化、男女の不平等の解消、若者への経済的支援やより良いワークライフ・バランスなど、具体的な対策を提案しており、それらを実現するには6兆円を超える財源が必要となる。日本の根本的な課題は、出生率の低下であり、我々は是非ともこの「子育て応援トータルプラン」を実現したいと思っている。岸田首相も、最近になってようやくこの問題の重要性に気づき、児童手当の拡充や0〜2歳のすべての子どもに対する毎年10万円の給付など、公明党の「子育て応援トータルプラン」に基づいて、「異次元」の子育て支援策を実現すると述べた。

　2022年9月27日に、私は公明党の政務調査会長を退任した。しかしながら、任期中に日本の重要課題に取り組み、その再生に道筋をつけることができた。2021年の衆議院総選挙では、公明党の主要政策が勝利をもたらした。また2022年の参議院選挙では、早稲田大学マニフェスト研究所は、公明党のマニフェストを全党の中で第1位に評価した。日本と世界の「激動の時代」の中で、人々の幸福と平和を目指し、様々な政策を実現するために全力を尽くしたことを誇りに

KOMEITO on September 25, 2022. However, I have tackled the crucial agendas of Japan and paved the way for the reconstruction during my tenure. In the 2021 general election, the major policies of the KOMEITO brought on the victory. The Waseda University Manifesto Research Institution evaluated the KOMEITO's Manifesto as the best one of all political parties for the 2022 House of Councillors election. I am proud of my best endeavors to realize various policies for the happiness of people and world peace amid turbulent times in Japan and around the world. I am convinced that the future of Japan will be bright. I would like to extend my profound gratitude to the Diet members, and the excellent staff members of the Policy Research Council for formulating the highest levels of policy, as well as all the people involved in supporting me such as the headquarter of the KOMEITO and the KOMEI Shimbun for the past two years.

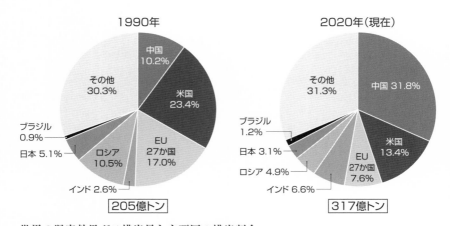

世界の温室効果ガス排出量と主要国の排出割合
出所：国際エネルギー機関（IEA）「Greenhouse Gas Emissions from Energy (2022)」「World Energy Outlook (2022)」等に基づいて環境省が作成

思う。日本の未来は明るいと確信する。2年に亘り、最高水準の政策を創り上げてくれた国会議員と政務調査会の優秀な職員の皆様、また党本部や公明新聞など私を支えて頂いたすべての関係者の方々に、心からの感謝を申し上げたい。

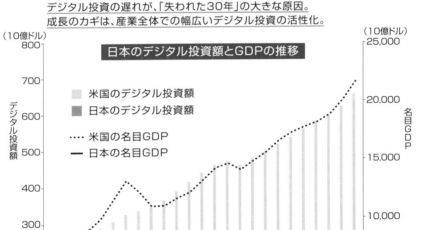

デジタル投資額とGDPの動きは、ほぼ連動しており、国全体における
デジタル投資の遅れが、「失われた30年」の大きな原因。
成長のカギは、産業全体での幅広いデジタル投資の活性化。

国全体におけるデジタル投資の長期低迷
注1：1ドル＝100円で計算
　　2：デジタル投資額はOECD Statに掲載されているハードウェア投資とソフトウェア投資の合計値
出所：経済協力開発機構（OECD）、内閣府、米国商務省を基に作成された「産業構造審議会　経済産業政策新機軸部会」第2回資料より

Two Election Defeats made me grow as a Statesman

I was born June 25, 1958, in Kyoto City, Japan.

In 1971, owing to intensive study, I had the good fortune of passing the entrance examination at St. Viator Rakusei Junior and Senior High School, one of the most prominent mission schools in Japan. When I was a first year student at the junior high school, I joined the school baseball club and until the third year of the senior high school, I had spent all my time playing baseball. During my senior high school days, our team went on to play in the quarterfinal round for Kyoto prefecture for the National High School Baseball Championship held every summer.

In 1978, I entered the law department of Kyoto University, majoring in administrative law. However, I not only studied law, but also politics, history, sociology, literature, philosophy, economics, public finance, science, and so on.

After graduation, I joined The Sanwa Bank, Ltd. (now The Mitsubishi UFJ Bank, Ltd.), as an executive trainee. I was engaged in various departments, such as loans, economic research, marketing, planning, and large urban development project. In 1990, I took office as acting director at the department of large urban developments.

In 1992, at 34 years of age, I was suddenly requested to run in the upcoming general election for the KOMEITO. I was very surprised at this request and terribly wavered whether to become a statesman or to succeed as a businessman. Finally, I made up my mind to enter the political world, because I found it important to work for public interests.

I was first elected as a member of the House of Representatives in 1993 from the First District of Kyoto Prefecture under a multi-seat electoral system. During my first term, I belonged to the

186

二度の選挙の敗北が、私を政治家として成長させた

1958年6月25日、私は京都市で生まれました。

1971年、猛勉強の末、運良くカトリックの聖ヴィアトール学園洛星中学校・高等学校の入学試験に合格できましたが、中学1年生の時から野球部に入部し、高校3年生の夏まで野球に明け暮れる生活を送っていました。高校時代には、夏の全国高校野球選手権大会・京都府予選の準々決勝に出場したこともあります。

1978年に京都大学法学部に入学し、3回生からは芝池教授の行政法ゼミに入りました。しかし、法律だけでなく政治学、歴史学、社会学、文学、哲学、経済学、財政学、科学などにも没頭していました。

卒業後は、三和銀行（現三菱UFJ銀行）に入行。融資、経済の調査・分析、マーケティング、企画、大規模都市開発プロジェクトなど、様々な部門に携わり、1990年には大規模都市開発部・部長代理に就任しました。

ところが、1992年、34歳の時、突然公明党から、次の総選挙に出馬するよう要請を受けたのです。私はこの要請に非常に驚き、政治家になるべきか、それともビジネスマンとして成功を目指すべきか迷いました。しかし、さんざん悩んだ末に、私は公共の利益のために働くことが大切であると感じ、政治の世界に入ることを決心いたしました。

1993年、中選挙区制のもとで、無事に京都府第1区から衆議院議員に初当選することができました。最初の任期中、私は大蔵委員会などに所属し、有望な論客として評価も頂きました。しかし、1996年の総選挙では、1994年に導入された小選挙区制のもとで、残念ながら議席を獲得できず落選となりました。敗北の原因は、私の政治家としての未熟さにありました。背景には、（中選挙区制から小選挙区への）選挙制度の変更や、公明党と新進党の合併、オウム真理教による地下鉄サ

standing committee on financial affairs and was recognized as a promising and controversial statesman. However, in the 1996 general election, I failed to win a seat in the single-seat district which had been introduced in 1994. The cause of this failure was mainly due to my inexperience as a politician. Against this backdrop, was a change in the election system, the integration of the KOMEITO and the New Frontier Party, and the Tokyo Subway Sarin Incident by the Aum Shinrikyo. It could be said that I was at the mercy of these political and social turbulences.

In 1999, I was elected as a member of the Kyoto City Assembly, Kamigyo District of Kyoto City. At that time, there was nobody else who had switched from a member of the Diet to a local assembly member.

To tell the truth, it was hard for me. However, it was fairly difficult for the KOMEITO to win a seat in the single-seat constituency, and so I decided to train myself as a statesman at the local assembly. In 2003, I was subsequently reelected as a member of the Kyoto City Assembly. The motto of the KOMEITO is "Stand with the people". Night and day, local assembly members totaling around 3,000 make every effort to hear the people, support the livelihoods of the people, and solve various agendas for their districts. I keenly realized that these local assembly members are the cornerstone of the KOMEITO and more crucial than Diet members for the poeple. A wise proverb from Japan says "Those who brighten up a dark corner of society are treasures for the nation". This applies to the local assembly members of the KOMEITO.

In 2005, another opportunity had presented itself. This time, I was requested to run for the general election again in the proportional representation system. However, I was defeated once again, due to the snap election by Prime Minister Koizumi on the privatization of the Japanese postal system and the landslide

リン事件などがあり、これらの政治的、社会的動乱に翻弄されたことも事実です。

　2年半の浪人生活の後、1999年には方針転換をして、京都市上京区から京都市議会議員に挑戦し当選いたしました。当時、国会議員から地方議員に転身した人は他にいませんでした。

　正直に言うと、この転身は私にとっては辛い決断でした。しかし、公明党が小選挙区で議席を獲得するのはかなり難しかったため、地方議会から政治家として自分を鍛え直すことにしたのです。その後も、2003年に京都市議会議員として再選されました。公明党のモットーは「大衆とともに」にあります。約3,000名に及ぶ地方議員が、日夜人々の声を聴き、人々の暮らしを支え、また地域の課題解決に献身的に奔走しているのです。私は、地方議員こそ党の基盤であり、大衆にとっては国会議員よりも、かけがえのない存在であると痛感しました。日本には「一隅を照らす、これ則ち国宝なり」という名言がありますが、公明党の地方議員こそ、まさに「国の宝」であると言えるでしょう。

　2005年、もう一度挑戦の機会が訪れました。今度は比例代表で、再び総選挙に出馬するよう要請され立候補したのです。ところが、自民党の小泉純一郎首相による、いわゆる郵政民営化を争点にした突然の解散と自民党の地滑り的勝利により、私は次点となり2度目の敗北を喫しました。

　天を仰ぎながら、私は心の底から落胆し、疲れ果て、絶望の淵にありました。しかし同時に、自分の業の深さを感じ、運命に試されていることを悟ったのです。現実をありのままに受け入れて、家族とともに次の勝利に向かって前に進むしかありませんでした。私は、4年間にわたり、ひたすら選挙区内の支持者を訪問し、人々の声を聞き、様々な要望や社会課題を調査するとともに、人々に支援を訴えました。

　その結果、2009年の衆議院選挙でようやく国会に戻ることとなりました。一方、自民党と公明党はこの選挙で大敗北し、民主党政権が誕

189

victory of the LDP.

In looking up to the heavens, I was really disappointed and exhausted, and at the brink of despair. At the same time, I felt the depth of my karma and realized that I was being put to the test by destiny. I had no choice but to accept reality and move forward pursuing victory with my family. I was determined to rise up and began to visit our supporters throughout my constituency, hearing people's voices, researching their various needs and social agendas, and appealing for their support for four years.

As a result, I was reelected as a member of the House of Representatives in 2009. Conversely, in this election, the LDP and KOMEITO were completely defeated by the Democratic Party of Japan, which rose to power. Thirteen years have passed since I lost my seat in the House of Representatives. To date, no other Diet member, except myself, has made a comeback after 13 years. I fully realized the importance of my mission, when I was 51 years of age.

While I had left the Diet for thirteen years, the book that encouraged me was "Representative Men of Japan / Japan and the Japanese" written by Mr. Kanzo UCHIMURA. This book is a biography of five great men (SAIGO Takamori, UESUGI Yozan, NINOMIYA Sontoku, NAKAE Toju, and NICHIREN) and taught me how political leaders should be. I deeply regretted what I had done and made up my mind to become a statesman and contribute to the people. It is no exaggeration to say that two election defeats and an experience as a local assembly member made me grow as a statesman.

I would like to express my profound gratitude to my wife Mayumi who had often saved me from crises, and those who had supported me to serve a mission during this hard time.

生したのです。私が衆議院の議席を失ってから13年の歳月が経っていました。当時は、日本の憲政史上、国会議員を経験した後、地方議員を経て国会議員に戻った人は、私以外にはいませんでした。自らの使命の重大さに気づかされました。私は51歳になっていました。

　私は13年もの長い間国会を離れていましたが、この間私を勇気づけてくれたのは、内村鑑三氏の著書『代表的日本人』でした。この本は日本を代表する5人の偉大な人物（西郷隆盛、上杉鷹山、二宮尊徳、中江藤樹、日蓮）の伝記で、政治指導者の在り方を教えてくれました。私は自分の行ってきたことを深く反省するとともに、改めて人々に貢献する政治家になることを決心したのです。二度の選挙での敗北と地方議員の経験が、政治家としての成長につながったと言っても過言ではありません。

　私が危機に陥った時に何度も助けてくれた妻や、私が最も苦しい時に支え、使命を与えてくださった皆様に、心からの感謝を申し上げたいと思います。

京都の支援者の皆様と選挙事務所にて
With my supporters, campaign office, Kyoto.

TAKEUCHI Yuzuru

Date of Birth: June 25, 1958
Birth Place: Kyoto Prefecture
Political Party: The KOMEITO
Member of the House of Representatives (6 terms)
Constituency: Kinki Proportional Representation Block

Education

March	1983	Faculty of Law, Kyoto University

Career

September	2022	Chairperson, Committee on Economy, Trade and Industry, HR
September	2021	Elected as a Member of the House of Representatives (6th)
September	2020	Chairperson, Policy Research Council of the KOMEITO
October	2019	Director of the Committee on Foreign Affairs, HR
October	2018	Secretary-General on Tax Committee of the KOMEITO
April	2018	Director of the Committee on Financial Affairs, HR
November	2017	Main members of the Taxation Council by the ruling coalition
October	2017	Elected as a Member of the House of Representatives (5th)
September	2016	Chairperson, Committee on Internal Affairs and Communication, HR
October	2015	The State Minister of Health, Labour and Welfare
December	2014	Elected as a Member of the House of Representatives (4th)
September	2014	Director of the House Steering Committee, HR

プロフィール

竹内　譲

生年月日：1958 年 6 月 25 日
出身：京都府
所属政党：公明党
衆議院議員（当選 6 回）
選挙区：比例代表近畿ブロック

学歴

1983 年　3 月　　京都大学法学部　卒業

経歴

2022 年　9 月　　衆議院経済産業委員長

2021 年　9 月　　衆議院選挙当選（6 回）

2020 年　9 月　　公明党政務調査会長

2019 年　10 月　　衆議院外務委員会理事

2018 年　10 月　　公明党税制調査会事務局長

2018 年　4 月　　衆議院財務金融委員会理事

2017 年　11 月　　与党税制協議会メンバー

2017 年　10 月　　衆議院選挙当選（5 回）

2016 年　9 月　　衆議院総務委員長

2015 年　10 月　　厚生労働副大臣

2014 年　12 月　　衆議院選挙当選（4 回）

2014 年　9 月　　衆議院議院運営委員会理事

September	2014	The First Vice Chairperson on Diet Policy Committee of the KOMEITO
October	2013	Director of the Committee on Financial Affairs, HR
December	2012	Parliamentary Secretary for Finance (Abe Cabinet)
December	2012	Elected as a Member of the House of the Representatives (3rd)
October	2010	Director of the Committee on Financial Affairs, HR
January	2010	Director of the Committee on Land, Infrastructure, Transport and Tourism, HR
October	2009	Chief Representative, the NEW KOMEITO Kyoto Prefectural Headquarters
August	2009	Director of the Special Committee on North Korea's abductions and other issues, HR
August	2009	Elected as a Member of the House of the Representatives (2nd)
April	2003	Reelected as a Member of the Kyoto City Assembly
April	1999	Elected as a Member of the Kyoto City Assembly
July	1993	Elected as a Member of the House of the Representatives (1st)
April	1983	Joined The Sanwa Bank Ltd. (The Bank of Mitsubishi UFJ, Ltd.)

HR = House of Representatives

Family

Wife, 2 children

My favorite book

"Representative Men of Japan / Japan and the Japanese"
by UCHIMURA Kanzo

Hobbies

Baseball, Singing, Go (Strategic board game)

2014 年	9 月	公明党国会対策委員会筆頭副委員長
2013 年	10 月	衆議院財務金融委員会理事
2012 年	12 月	財務大臣政務官（安倍内閣）
2012 年	12 月	衆議院選挙当選（3 回）
2010 年	10 月	衆議院財務金融委員会理事
2010 年	1 月	衆議院国土交通員会理事
2009 年	10 月	公明党京都府本部代表就任
2009 年	8 月	衆議院北朝鮮による拉致問題等に関する特別委員会理事
2009 年	8 月	衆議院選挙当選（2 回）
2003 年	4 月	京都市会議員選挙再選
1999 年	4 月	京都市会議員選挙当選
1993 年	7 月	衆議院選挙当選（1 回）
1983 年	4 月	三和銀行（現三菱 UFJ 銀行）に就職

家族

妻、子供 2 人

愛読書

『代表的日本人』内村鑑三著

趣味

野球、ボーカル、囲碁

Turbulent Times for Japanese Politics

激動 日本の政治
<small>げきどう　にほん　せいじ</small>

2023 年 8 月 1 日　初版発行

著　者　竹内　譲／TAKEUCHI Yuzuru

制作・発売　**中央公論事業出版**
〒 101-0051　東京都千代田区神田神保町 1-10-1
IVY ビル 5 階
電話　03-5244-5723
URL　https://www.chukoji.co.jp/

印刷　藤原印刷
製本　松岳社
装丁　studio TRAMICHE